Mary Potter

Poetry of Nature

Comprising, a selection of the most sublime and beautiful apostrophes, histories,

songs, elegies, &c. from the works of the Caledonian bards.

Mary Potter

Poetry of Nature
Comprising, a selection of the most sublime and beautiful apostrophes, histories, songs, elegies, &c. from the works of the Caledonian bards.

ISBN/EAN: 9783337329433

Printed in Europe, USA, Canada, Australia, Japan

Cover: Foto ©Thomas Meinert / pixelio.de

More available books at **www.hansebooks.com**

POETRY

OF

NATURE,

COMPRISING,

A SELECTION OF THE MOST

SUBLIME AND *BEAUTIFUL*

APOSTROPHES,	SONGS,
HISTORIES,	ELEGIES, &c.

FROM THE WORKS

OF THE

CALEDONIAN BARDS.

The TYPOGRAPHICAL Execution in a Style entirely New,
and Decorated with the Superb Ornaments,
of the Celebrated Caslon.

(Price Ten Shillings and Six-Pence.)

LIST of SUBSCRIBERS.

HIS Grace the Duke of Leeds, * *St. James's-Square* 12 Copies

Right Hon. Lord Scarfdale, *Mansfield-ftreet, Portland-place*

Right Hon. Earl of Stanhope, *Ditto*

Right Hon. Lord Barrington, *Cavendifh-fquare*

Right Hon. Lord Wentworth, *Wimpole-ftreet*

Right Rev. Lord Bifhop of St. David's, *Upper Seymour street*

Lady Bernard, *Portland-place* 2 Copies

Sir Thomas Skipwith, Bart. *Harley-ftreet*

Sir Henry George Liddel, Bart. *Upper Harley-ftreet* 2 Copies

Sir Matthew White Ridley, *Portland-place*

Sir William Burrell, *Harley-ftreet*

Lady Burrell, *Ditto*

Sir Gregory Page Turner, Bart. *Portland-place*

General Smith, *Harley-ftreet*

James Sibbald, Efq; *Upper Harley-ftreet*

Samuel Johnftone, Efq; *Ditto*

Samuel

* It is neceffary to obferve this was the late Duke, and that his patronage for this Work was obtained a very fhort time before his deceafe.

Samuel Parke, Efq; *Moore-place, Lambeth*
Mrs. Finch, *Cavendifh-fquare*
Samuel Whitbread, Efq; *Wimpole-ftreet*
Vice Admiral Darby, *Cavendifh fquare*
James Clayton, Efq; *Ditto*   2 Copies
Henry Maxwell, Efq; *Harley-ftr. Cavendifh-fqu.*
William Shard, Efq; *Upper Harley-ftreet*
Samuel Penn, Efq; *Somerfet-ftreet, Portman-fqu.*
Frederick Pigou, Efq; *Wimpole-ftr. Cavendifh-fqu.*
Adam Afkew, Efq; *Wimpole-ftreet*
Ralph Ward, Efq; *Ditto*
Mr. Richardfon, *Upper Wimpole-ftreet*
John Purling, Efq; *Portland-place*
Capt. Mercer, *Queen-Ann-ftreet, Weft*
Lieut. Gen. Baugh, *Wimpole-ftreet*
Charles Turner, Efq; *Ditto*
W. Higginfon, Efq; *Harley-ftreet*
Warren Haftings, Efq; *Wimpole-ftreet,*
Mr. Grant, *Tower-Hill*
Jofeph Yorke, Efq; *Portland-place*
Mifs Yorke, *Ditto*
James Revel Frye, Efq; *Wimpole-ftreet*
Mr. Hampfon, *Wimpole-ftreet*   2 Copies
                                        Thomas

Thomas Fitzhugh, Efq; *Portland-place,* 2 Copies
Capt. Cornifh, *Charlotte-ftreet, Portland-place*
Mr. J. Daniell, *Welbeck-ftreet*
William Pigou, Efq; *Portland-place*
George Romney, Efq; *Cavendifh-fquare*
Vice Admiral Digby, *Upper Harley-ftreet*
Mr. Lamar, *Welbeck-street*
John Baker, Efq ; *Ditto*
Mrs. Campbell, *Mortimer-ftreet*
Mrs. Salwey, *ditto*
Mr. Douglafs, *New Cavendifh-street*
John Ellis, Efq; *Berkeley-street, Manchefter-fqu.*
Col. Morfe, *Dutchefs-street, Portland-place*
Mrs. Steele, *Bentinck-street, Portman-fquare*
John Jones, Efq; *Mortimer-street*
Lawrence La Foreft, Efq; *Manchester-fquare*
Charles Selwyn, Efq; *Duke-street, ditto*
Mrs. Welch, *Berkeley-street, ditto*
Lt. Col. Mercer, *Royal Engineers, Duke-street,*
  Manchester-fquare
Mifs Doleman, *ditto*
Mifs Dubourgh, *ditto*

Mr.

Mr. Gordon, *Manchester-square*
James Delancy, Efq; *Edwards-str. Portman-squ.*
William Ottley, Efq; *Margaret-street*
Col. Symes, *Holles-street*
Mrs. Hardinge, *Wigmore-street*
Charles Boone, Efq; *Portman-fquare*
Mr. Martin, *Somerfet-street*
Stephen Beckingham, *Efq*; *Portman-fquare*
Lieut. Col. Doyle, *Bryanstone-street*
General Paoli, *Upper Seymour-street*
Mrs. S. Wyndham, *Queen Ann-street, West*
George Mercer, *Efq*; *Margaret-street*
Mrs. Gardener, *ditto*
Capt. Marfhall, *Holles-street*
Archibald Cochran, *Efq*; *Great Cumberland str.*
Col. Bullock, *Berkelev street, Manchester square*
R. Nafmith, *Efq*; *Great Titchfield street*
Mrs. Oram, *Wimpole street*
Mrs. Catherine Lockwood, *Henrietta street*
—— Lovedon, *Efq*; *Stratford place*

PRELIMINARY ADDRESS.

THE flattering reception given by the World to innumerable Compilations from the Works of the most approved Modern Authors, under the captivating title of their Beauties; should seem to warrant a probability that an apology for the following Attempt would scarcely be necessary. Religion, Morality, Metaphysics, Philosophy, Poetry, and even History, has been repeatedly employed for this purpose; whether such display of the art of Book-making has been more beneficial to the Authors, the Booksellers, or the Public, does not become the Editor of the ensuing pages to determine. The prime intent of the present production is to introduce for public inspection, a species of Typographical Elegance as yet very little (if at all) known; and it was necessary, to chuse the method and matter sufficiently eligible, as well to display the beauties of the performance, as to render it productive of the benevolent purpose it is designed to answer.

The Editor reprobates the idea of insinuating a wish, that this Selection may be considered as superseding the Works of the Caledonian Bards, or even comprehending all their beauties and excellencies: Her best hopes are only, that the principal Episodes, Addresses, &c. will be more interesting to the Reader, and easier

retained

*retained in the Memory than when attached to Matter less conse-
quential, and encumbered with a perpetual iteration of the same
allusions and images.*

*Every Admirer of pure Heroism, exalted Sentiment, delicate
Affection, and strong marked Character, must be lovers of the
Galic Poetry; and with these the Editor flatters herself if she
does not aspire to the expectancy of Praise, she will incur no great
degree of censure, by presenting it in a form at least Novel, and in
a stile of Typographical Superiority as yet unattemped.*

*Never so happy as when an oppertunity presents, to testify the
sincerest acknowledgments of a grateful heart: the Editor cannot
omit embracing the present, by intreating the numerous Subscribers
to the posthumous publications of the late Mr. Potter her Father,
to accept (as the only possible return in her power, for such unpre-
cented goodness) her earnest wishes, that they may be ever in
possession of those exquisitely delightful feelings which animate the
bosom of sensibility, whose greatest luxury is the participation of woes
not immediately its own; and whose supreme pleasure is relieving
them.———*

January 26th.
1789.

CONTENTS

CONTENTS

AND

EXPLANATORY NOTES.

OURD.—The *Ourd* is the trunk of a large tree, set on fire, round which the *Highlanders* solemnize peculiar festivals; a custom rigidly observed at this day in many parts of the Country.

ALBIN.—This word signifies a Mountainous Country, and seems once to have been the name of all the Island: but after the *Saxons* had defeated the *South Britains,* and became masters of that division; such of them as maintained their independancy, were honoured with the appelation of *Ualsh,* or *Nobility,* in opposition to the vulgar, who submitted to the

the conquerors; and the northern divifion, comprehending all *Scotland*, has been fince invariably known by the name of A L B I N.

CO M P L A I N T of the B A R D.   Page 3

T o s c A R, father of M A L V I N A, to the latter of which this Complaint is addreffed by O s s i A N, as are many other of his tendereft compofitions : She appears to have been in love with O s c A R, the fon of O s s i A N, and to have affected the company of the *Father* after the death of the *Son*.

C O N A.—O s s i A N the fon of F i N G A L is often poetically called, the voice of C o N A.

M A L V I N A.—*Soft or lovely brow.*

S O N G of C O L M A.   Page 6

C O L M A.—*A Woman with fine Hair.*

D E A T H of M O R N A.   Page 10

M O R N A.—*A Woman univerfally beloved.*

E R I N.—As the names of *Lochlin, Erin,* and *Inis-fail* often occur in thefe Poems, it may be proper to remember, that by *Lochlin* is meant N o R w A y, or S c A N D I N A V I A in general, by *Erin,* I R E L A N D, and by *Inis-fail,* a part of the fame Country, inhabited by the *Falans* (whence *Inis-fail.)*——— Sometimes *Inis-fail* feems to denote fome of the H E B R I D E S ; and *Iniftore* ftands always for the O R K N E y s, or at leaft the greateft part of them : it may be alfo proper to obferve the footing which the kings of *Morven* or C A L E D O N I A were with

with thefe neighbouring countries. With the inhabitants of *Inis-fail* and *Iniftore*, they generally lived on good terms; and feem to have been their fuperiors. With the legal fovereigns of *Erin* and their people, they were nearly allied; and frequently affifted them againft the ufurpations of the *Firbolg*, and the incurfions of the *Scandinavians*; with their fouthern neighbours, beyond the friths of *Forth* and *Clyde*, the kings of *Morven* feem to have had very little friendly intercourfe.

CAIRBAR.—*Strong-Man.*————GOLBUN.—*Crooked-Hill.*

L U B A R.—*A river in the province of Ulfter.*

B R A S S O L I S.—*White-Breafted.*

C R O M L A.—*The proper name of a hill on the coaft of Ulfter.*

T R E N M O R—*Tall and Mighty*, the great Grand-Father of F i n g a l.

M O R V E N—All the north-weft coaft of *Scotland* went of old under the name of *Morven*, which fignifies a ridge of *very* high hills.

F I N G A L—Son of Comhal and Morna the daughter of Thaddu, his Grand-father was Trathal, and great Grand-father Trenmor, both of which are often mentioned in the *Galic Poetry*.

Moral

This is often called the song of the children of MURNO: it will be neceſſary to remember that *Arden* was his father, *Torman* his bard, and *Dunalva* his place of reſidence.

V I N V E L A—*A Woman with a melodious voice.*

B R A N N O ſignifies a *Mountain-ſtream,* and is a river known by that name in the days of OSSIAN; there are ſeveral ſmall rivers in *Scotland* ſtill retains this name; in particular one which falls into the *Tay.*

CORMORA—*high rocky hill.*—CRONNAN—*mournful ſound.*
He

He faw her fair moving on the plain.——The diftinction which the *ancient Scots* made between good and bad Spirits, was, that the *former* appeared fometimes in the day time, in lonely unfrequented places; but the *latter* never but by night, and in a difmal and gloomy fcene.

CUL-ALIN—Of *Cul*, a poetical name for a Lady's fine locks; and *alin*, graceful.——The name of *Allan*, or *Allen* in *Scotland* and *Ireland* is from the fame root.

CRACA—*Probably one of the Shetland Ifles.*

When the darknefs of thy countenance grows.——The Poet means the *Moon in her wane*; this addrefs in the original is in a lyric meafure, and appears to have been fung to the harp

MOINA—*Soft in perfon and temper.*——CLUTHA—the river *Clyde*, the fignification of the word is *bending*, alluding to the winding courfe of that river.

Darthula

DARTHULA—*A Woman with fine Eyes.*——She was the moſt famous beauty of antiquity, and to this day it is a common phraſe, " *as lovely as Darthula.*"

GAUL *the Son of Morni,* was a diſtinguiſhed character in the wars of FINGAL, and of courſe much noticed in the Poems of OSSIAN.

DERMID *Son of Duina*—This perſonage is frequently mentioned in other poems of OSSIAN, and much celebrated in the Tales of *later times*

SELMA—This word in the original ſignifies either *beautiful to behold,* or a place *with a pleaſant or wide proſpect.* In thoſe times they built their houſes upon eminences, to command a view of the country, and to prevent their being ſurprized.

TEMORA—*The royal palace of the ſupreme kings of Ireland.*

CATHULA king of *Iniſtore,* properly *Inniſ-ore,* or *Orc Innis,* " the iſle of *Whales,*" or *Orkneys,* the word *orc* is uſed in this ſenſe by Milton.
———————— An iſland ſalt and bare,
The haunt of ſeals, and *orcs,* and ſea mews c'ang.

Heroiſm

The heroes of this piece are OSCAR the fon of CARUTH, and DERMID the fon of DIARAN; OSSIAN, (or perhaps his Imitator) opens the poem with a lamentation for OSCAR, and afterwards by an eafy tranfition, relates the ftory of OSCAR, the fon of CARUTH, who feems to have bore a character equally great, as well as the name of OSCAR, the fon of OSSIAN.

CREYLA—*the woody rock,* fuppofedto be one of the *Grampian Hills,* which ftill retains that name.—It was cuftomary for every great family to have a fecret cave, or place of concealment from their enemies, when they were forced to fly in Battle.

INVER, fignifies a place where a lefter river joins a greater, or empties itfelf into the ocean. All the towns in Scotland, whofe names begin with *Inver,* are thus fituated, as Invernefs Inver-ary, Inver-keithing, &c.———DUNGEAL—*White Tower.* The houfe of Dungeal are faid to have been the progenitors of the *Cummings,* lords of *Badenoch,* whofe tranf-actions are fo well known in the hiftory of Scotland.———

SULGORMA—*Blue-Eyed*———BENVEL—*Sweet-Voiced.*

MALALIN—*Graceful Eye-brow.*———ERVIN — *Weftern Hill.*———

Ronnan

RONNAN—from Ro, thonnan—*through waves.*

TRATHAL—This hero was grand-Father to FINGAL, and
generalliffimo of the *Caledonian* Army in their wars with the
Romans; there is frequent mention made of him in the other
Poems of OSSIAN.

MAC-THALLA—*Son of the Rock,* the Galic name for Echo.

ORAN-MOLLA—*A Song of Praife.*

So great was the attachment of the *ancient Caledonians* to their
hills, that we often find them, not only taking a folemn farewell of them at death, but alfo imagining that a part of their
future happinefs confifted in feeing and travelling over thofe
fcenes, which in life afforded them fo much pleafure.

* Errata in this Article, page 162, for Chief of Scarlaw, read Fall of Tura.

APOSTROPHE

APOSTROPHE to OSSIAN.

O Ofsian, king of songs! thou who drew the tear from the eye: Thou who brought the foe to the ground!——Royal mourner of Selma's race! where shall I search for thy tomb? The sons of negligence have suffered the waving heath to cover it.——The hearer of tales round the burning oud meets thy words; and he melts before them.——The course of the storm is abroad; but thy tomb it meets not. The voice of its rage is aloud amongst the projecting cliffs: But thy narrow dwelling, O king of bards! it pafses over in silence. No huge stones rears its lofty head there, to compel the flying winds to stop their rapid journey, and, with murmuring accents, salute the mighty that

B   lie

lie below.——But roll on, voice of the north! the fame of Ossian regards thee not:——Thyself art but for a season. Tho' the feeble branches of the wood bend before thee, and the waving heath kneels at thy approach, when thou art gone, they erect their heads, and forget thy strength.===But the strength of Ossian's song shall never be forgot, while the oaks of Albin blaze before the tenants of her glens.

Chief of Scarlaw

Complaint

COMPLAINT of the BARD.

Darkness comes on my soul, O fair daughter of Toscar, I behold not the form of my son at Carun; nor the figure of Oscar on Crona.——The rustling winds have carried him far away; and the heart of his father is sad. But lead me O Malvina, to the sound of my woods; to the roar of my mountain streams.——Let the chace be heard on Cona; let me think on the days of other years. And bring me the harp, O maid, that I may touch it, when the light of my soul shall arise. Be thou near, to learn the song; future times shall hear of me! The sons of the feeble hereafter will lift the voice on Cona; and looking up to the rocks, say, "here Ossian dwelt." They shall admire the chiefs of old, and the race that are

B 2

no more! while we ride on our clouds, Malvina, on the wings of the roaring winds. Our voices shall be heard, at times, in the desert; we shall sing on the breeze of the rock.

Come thou beam that art lonely, from watching in the night! The squally winds are around thee, from all their echoing hills. Red, over my hundred streams, are the light covered paths of the dead. They rejoice, on the eddying winds, in the season of night. Dwells there not joy in song, while hand of the harps of Lutha? Awake the voice of the string; roll my soul to me. It is a stream that has failed. Malvina pour the song.

I hear thee, from thy darkness, in Selma, thou that watchest lonely, by night! why didst thou with hold the song, from Ofsians failing soul? as the falling brook to the ear of the hunter, descending from his storm=
covered

covered hill; in a sun=beam rolls the echoing stream; he hears, and shakes his dimy locks: such is the voice of Lutha, to the friend of the spirits of heroes. My swelling bosom beats high. I look back on the days that are past. Come, thou beam that art lonely from watching in the night.

Bring, daughter of Toscar, bring the harp! the light of the song rises in Ossian's soul! It is like the field, when darkness covers the hills around, and the shadow grows slowly on the plain of the sun. I behold my son, O Malvina, near the mossy rock of Crona. But it is the mist of the desert, tinged with the beam of the west! Lovely is the mist that assumes the form of Oscar! turn from it, ye winds, when ye roar on the side of Ardven.

Cathlin of Clutha. War of Caros.

Song

SONG of COLMA.

It is night; I am alone, forlorn on the hill of storms. The wind is heard in the mountains. The torrent pours down the rock. No hut receives me from the rain; forlorn on the hill of winds! Rise, Moon! from behind thy clouds. Stars of the night arise, lead me, some light, to the place, where my love rests from the chace alone! His bow near him unstrung: his dogs panting around him.——But here I must sit alone, by the rock of the mossy stream. The stream and the wind roar aloud. I hear not the voice of my love! Why delays my Salgar, why the chief of the hills, his promise? Here is the rock, and here the tree! here is the roaring stream! Thou didst promise with night to be here. Ah! whether is my

Salgar

Salgar gone? with thee I would fly, from my father; with thee, from my brother of pride. Our race have long been foes; we are not foes, O Salgar! Cease a little while, O wind! stream be thou silent a while! let my voice be heard around, let my wanderer hear me! Salgar! it is Colma who calls. Here is the tree, and the rock, Salgar my love! I am here. Why delayest thou thy coming? lo! the calm moon comes forth.——The flood is bright in the vale.——The rocks are grey on the steep.——I see him not on the brow.——His dogs come not before him, with tidings of his near approach.——Here I must sit alone!

Who lies on the heath beside me? Are they my love and my brother? Speak to me O my friends! To Colma they give no reply.——Speak to me: I am alone! My soul is tormented with fears! Ah! they are dead! Their swords are red from the fight.——O my brother!

brother! my brother! why hast thou slain my Salgar?
Why, O Salgar! hast thou slain my brother? Dear
were ye both to me! What shall I say in your praise?
Thou wert fair on the hill among thousands! He
was terrible in fight.——Speak to me; hear my voice,
hear me, sons of my love! They are silent: silent for
ever.——Cold, cold are their breasts of clay! oh!
from the rock on the hill; from the top of the windy
steep, speak, ye ghosts of the dead! speak, I will
not be afraid! whither are ye gone to rest? in what
cave of the hill shall I find the departed? No
feeble voice is on the gale: no answer half-drowned in
the storm!

I sit alone in my grief! I wait for morning
in my tears! rear the tomb, ye friends of the dead.
Close it not till Colma comes.——My life flies away
like a dream: why should I stay behind? Here
shall

shall I rest with my friends, by the stream of the sounding rock.——When night comes on the hill; when the loud winds arise; my ghost shall stand in the blast, and mourn the death of my friends. The hunter shall hear from his booth.——He shall fear but love my voice! for sweet shall my voice be for my friends: pleasant were her friends to Colma!

Songs of Selma.

C   Death

DEATH of MORNA.

———

" Cathba fell by the sword of Duchomar at the oak of the noisy streams.——Duchomar came to Tura's cave; he spoke to lovely Morna. Morna, fairest among women, lovely daughter of strong=armed Cormac! why in the circle of stones? in the cave of the rock alone? The stream murmurs along. The old tree groans in the wind. The lake is troubled before thee; dark are the clouds of the sky! But thou art snow on the heath; thy hair is the mist of Cromla; when it curls on the hill; when it shines to the beam of the west! Thy breasts are two smooth rocks seen from Branno of streams. Thy arms like two white pillars, in the halls of the great Fingal."

" From whence Duchomar, most gloomy of men?

dark

dark are thy brows and terrible! Red are thy rolling eyes! does Swaran appear on the sea? what of the foe Duchomar?"——" From the hill I return O Morna, from the hill of the dark=brown hinds. Three have I slain with my bended yew. Three with my long bounding dogs of the chace.——Lovely daughter of Cormac, I love thee as my soul! I have slain one stately deer for thee.——High was his branchy head; and fleet his feet of wind."——" Duchomar!" calm the maid, replied, I love thee not, thou gloomy man! hard is thy heart of rock; dark is thy terrible brow. But Cathba young son of Torman, thou art the love of Morna. Thou art a sun=beam, in the day of the gloomy storm. Sawest thou the son of Torman, lovely on the hill of his hinds? Here the daughter of Cormac, waits the coming of Cathba!"

 " Long shall Morna wait," Duchomar said,

" long

" long shall Morna wait for Cathba! Behold this
sword unsheathed! here wanders the blood of Cathba.
Long shall Morna wait. He fell by the stream of
Branno! On Croma I will raise his tomb,
daughter of blue-shielded Cormac! Turn on Duchomar
thy eyes; his arm is strong as a storm."——" Is the
son of Torman fallen?" said the wildly bursting
voice of the maid. " Is he fallen on his echoing hills,
the youth with the breast of snow? the first in the
chace of hinds? the foe of the strangers of ocean?
Thou art dark, to me, Duchomar, cruel is thy arm to
Morna! Give me that sword my foe! I love the
wandering blood of Cathba.

He gave the sword to her tears. She pierced his
manly breast! He fell, like the bank of a mountain
stream, and stretching forth his hand, he spoke.
" Daughter of blue=shielded Cormac! thou hast slain

me

me in youth! The sword is cold to my breast: Morna,
I feel it cold. Give me to Moina the maid.
Duchomar was the dream of her night! she will raise
my tomb; the hunter shall raise my fame.——But
draw the sword from my breast, Morna, the steel
is cold!" She came, in all her tears, she came; she
drew the sword from his breast. He pierced her
white side! he spread her fair locks on the ground!
Her bursting blood sounds from her side: her white
arm is stained with red. Rolling in death she lay.
The cave re-echoed to her sighs."——

" Peace" said Cuthullin, "to the souls of the
heroes! their deeds were great in fight. Let them
ride around me on clouds. Let them shew their
features of war. My soul shall then be firm in
danger; mine arm like the thunder of heaven! But
be thou on a moon=beam, O Morna! near the window

of

of my r t; when my thoughts are of peace; when the din of arms is past. Gather the strength of the tribes! Move to the wars of Erin! Attend the car of my battles! rejoice in the noise of my course! place three spears by my side: follow the bounding of my steeds! That my soul may be strong in my friends, when battle darkens round the beams of my steel.

Fingal.

The

The Story of CAIRBAR and GRUDAR.

In other days came the sons of ocean to Erin! A thousand vessels bounded on waves to Ullins lovely plains. The sons of Inis=fail arose, to meet the race of dark-brown shields. Cairbar, first of men, was there, and Grudar, stately youth! Long had they strove for the spotted bull that lowed on Golbuns echoing heath. Each claimed him as his own. Death was often at the point of their steel! side by side the heroes fought; the strangers of ocean fled. Whose name was fairer on the hill, than the name of Cairbar and Grudar!——But ah! why ever lowed the Bull, on Golbun's echoing heath. They saw him leaping like snow. The wrath of the chiefs returned!

"On Lubars grassy banks they fought; Grudar fell

fell in his blood. Fierce Cairbar came to the vale, where Brassolis, fairest of his sisters, all alone, raised the song of grief. She sung of the actions of Grudar, the youth of her secret soul!——She mourned him in the field of blood; but still she hoped for his return. Her white bosom is seen from her robe, as the moon from the clouds of night, when its edge heaves white on the view, from the darkness, which covers its orb. Her voice was softer than the harp to raise the song of grief. Her soul was fixed on Grudar. The secret look of her eye was his.——
" When shalt thou come in thy arms thou mighty in war?"——

" Take Brassolis," Cairbar came and said " take Brassolis, this shield of blood. Fix it on high within my hall, the armour of my foe! Her soft heart beat against her side.——Distracted, pale, she flew.

flew. She found her youth in all his blood; she died on Cromla's heath. Here rests their dust Cuthullin. These lonely yews sprung from their tombs, and shade them from the storm. Fair was Brassolis on the plain! Stately was Grudar on the hill! The bard shall preserve their names, and send them down to future times!"

Fingal.

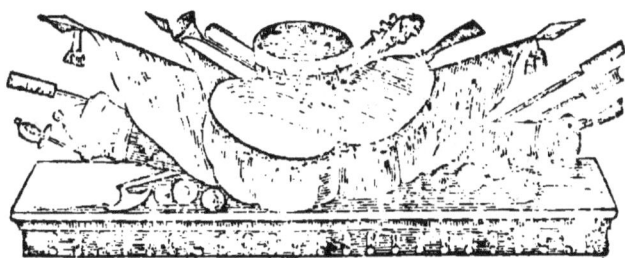

D   Trenmor.

TRENMOR.

"Trenmor" said the mouth of songs, lived in the days of other years. He bounded over the waves of the north: companion of the storm! The high rocks of the land of Lochlin; and its groves of murmuring sounds appeared to the hero through the mist:——He bound his white-bosomed sails.——Trenmor pursued the boar, that roared through the woods of Germal. Many had fled from its presence: but it rolled in death on the spear of Trenmor. Three Chiefs who beheld the deed, told of the mighty stranger. They told that he stood, like a pillar of fire, in the bright arms of his valour. The king of Lochlin prepared the feast. He called the blooming Trenmor. Three days he feasted at Germal's windy towers; and

received

received his choice in the combat. The land of Lochlin had no hero, that yielded not to Trenmor. The shell of joy went round with songs, in praise of the king of Morven. He that came over the waves, the first of mighty men.

Now when the fourth gray morn arose, the hero launched his ship. He walked along the silent shore, and called for the rushing wind: for loud and distant he heard the blast murmuring behind the groves. Covered over with arms of steel, a son of the woody Gormal appeared. Red was his cheek and fair his hair. His skin like the snow of Morven. Mild rolled his blue and smiling eyes, when he spoke to the king of swords.

" Stay, Trenmor, stay thou first of men, thou hast not conquered Lonval's son. My sword has often met the brave. The wise shun the strength

D 2

of

of my bow." "Thou fair-haired youth," Trenmor replied, " I will not fight with Lonval's son. Thine arm is feeble sun-beam of youth. Retire to Gormal's dark-brown hinds."——" But I will retire," replied the youth, " with the sword of Trenmor ; and exult in the sound of my fame. The virgins shall gather with smiles, around him who conquered mighty Trenmor. They shall sigh with the sighs of love, and admire the length of thy spear ; when I shall carry it among thousands ; when I lift the glittering point to the sun.

" Thou shalt never carry away my spear," said the angry king of Morven"——Thy mother shall find thee pale on the shore, and looking over the dark-blue deep, see the sails of him that slew her son. " I will not lift the spear," replied the youth, " my arm is not strong with years : but with the feathered dart,

I have

I have learned to pierce a distant foe. Throw down that heavy mail of steel. Trenmor is covered from death.—I first will lay my mail on earth.—Throw now thy dart, thou king of Morven!" He saw the heaving of her breast. It was the sister of the king.—She had seen him in the hall; and loved his face of youth.—The spear dropt from the hand of Trenmor: he bent his red cheek to the ground.—She was to him a beam of light that meets the sons of the cave; when they revisit the fields of the sun, and bend their aching eyes!—" Chief of the windy Morven," begun the maid with the arms of snow. " Let me rest in thy bounding ship, far from the love of Corlo. for he, like the thunder of the desart is terrible to Inibaca: he loves me in the gloom of pride. He shakes ten thousand spears!"—" Rest thou in peace," said the mighty Trenmor; " rest behind the shield

of

of my fathers.   I will not fly from the chief,   tho'
he shakes ten thousand spears!   Three days he waited
on the shore.   He sent his horn abroad.   He call'd
Corlo to battle, from all his echoing hills.   But
Corlo came not to battle.——The king of Lochlin
descends from his hall'.   He feasted on the roaring
shore.   He gave the maid to Trenmor.

Fingal.

Death

DEATH of ALDO.

"Who comes" said Fingal, " like the bounding roe, like the hart of echoing Cona? His shield glitters on his side, the clang of his armour is mournful.——He meets with Errayon in the strife! Behold the battle of the chiefs!——It is like the contending of ghosts in a gloomy storm.——But fallest thou son of the hill, and is thy white bosom stained with blood? Weep, unhappy Lorma, Aldo is no more! " The king took the spear of his strength. He was sad for the fall of Aldo. He bent his deathful eyes on the foe: but Gaul met the king of Sora.——Who can relate the fight of the chiefs?——The mighty stranger fell!

Lorma sat in Aldo's hall. She sat by the light

of

of a flaming oak. The night came down, but he did not return. The soul of Lorma is sad.——What detains thee, hunter of Cona? Thou didst promise to return.——Has the deer been distant far? do the dark winds sigh, round thee on the heath? I am in the land of strangers, where is my friend but Aldo? Come from thy sounding hill, O my best beloved.

Her eyes are turned towards the gate. She listens to the rustling blast. She thinks it is Aldo's tread. Joy rises in her face!——But sorrow returns again, like a thin cloud on the moon.——"Wilt thou not return my love? let me behold the face of the hill. The morn is in the east. Calm and bright is the breast of the lake? When shall I behold his dogs, returning from the chase? When shall I hear his voice, loud and distant on the wind? come from thy sounding hills, hunter of woody Cona!" His thin

ghost

ghost appeared, on a rock, like a watry beam of feeble light: when the moon rushes sudden from between two clouds, and the mid=night shower is on the field! She followed the empty form over the heath. She knew that her hero fell.——I heard her approaching cries on the wind, like the mournful voice of the breeze, when it sighs on the grafs of the cave!

She came. She found her hero! Her voice was heard no more. Silent she rolled her eyes. She was pale and wildly sad! Few were her days on Cona. She sunk into the tomb. Fingal commanded his bards; they sung over the death of Lorma. The daughters of Morven mourned her, for one day in the year, when the dark winds of autumn returned.

Son of the distant land! Thou dwellest in the field of fame! O let thy song arise, at times, in praise of those who fell. Let their thin ghosts rejoice around

E

thee;

thee; and the soul of Lorma come on a feeble beam: when thou liest down to rest, and the moon looks into thy cave. Then shalt thou see her lovely; but the tear is still on her check!

Silent and slow on floating mist; high hovering on the verge of the ocean, come ye ghosts of the dead! Ye bards of the times of old, here resume your employment, mourn the death of the lovely.——She merited the voice of your song.

Batt's of Lora.

Moralt

MORALT and MINVAS.

Let heroes who expect their tombs to rise by the white-armed daughters of beauty, said the bearer of Dunairm's shield, rest till morning; but Moralt shall fall amid the shades of night. No tomb of mine shall rise: No tear from the lovely shall bathe it. None shall lament over me, saying. ' Oh my hero!'——None shall lament over me, saying, ' Oh my son!' My arrow hath pierced the breast of the lovely: My spear is stained with the blood of my kindred.

My fathers were the foes of Albin. Their spears rose with Lochlins king. I longed to travel upon the waves of ocean. Six warriors raised my white sails. The wind came in haste from the north:

Waves

Waves gathered strength from the blast. Seas mingled with clouds that hurried along the face of the deep. The high hills of Albin rose on the top of the waves. The green woods of Sliavan shook their locks before the bounding of our bark.

The hall of Dunairm was the home of strangers. The gray haired chief stretched forth the hand of friendship to receive us. Welcome, said he, are the sons of ocean when they come in peace. Our deers are many: Our shells are full. The tales of our bards are pleasant; and why should the stranger mourn in our hall?

The feast was spread with mirth, and we blessed the foes of our fathers.

Minvas shone in the hall of her father, like the first beam of the rising sun, when it smiles on the dewy plains. Many chiefs sought the love of the maid;

maid; but she turned her eyes from the mighty, and fixed them on Moralt.

Nor hills, nor warriors were mine. I went to the battle alone. The foes of Lochlin had fallen by my hand; but my fame was not heard.

Go, said the maid; fight the battles of other kings. Gather thy fame in a distant land; send it before thee to Minvas, and she will own thy love.

I went to Erin's king. Many of his foes fell by my sword. My name was heard in song, and my fame travelled over many seas. The daughters of Inis=fail spread their white arms before me in vain. When peace smiled on the land, I returned to the maid of snow.

The sun lay asleep, and the moon wandered from cloud to cloud, when the hall of Dunairm appeared. From the skirts of a birchen grove, the breeze of

night

night conveyed to my ears a sound soft as the breath of summer.——'Go; and, if thou fall, Minvas will bathe thy sweet memory with her tears.'

My soul, that never trembled before, shook with dread and horror. I saw Minvas; and stately was the warrior who stood by her side.

I bent my bow.——Go, said I to an arrow, pierce that breast of falshood. Let no other warrior search for fame to please that heart of pride.

The steel entered her white bosom. Her variegated garment is spread on the heath. Her long hair is bathed in her blood. Her groans are mingled with the sighs of night.

Whence came the meteor of death, cried the warrior?——From an arm of strength I replied; and raised my spear.

Son of gloomy night, said the astonished youth, thy

thy arm is strong because the foe was feeble. The spear of the mighty never rose before a dark heart like thine. But thy surly ghost shall forthwith depart from its dwelling, and mingle with the sons of the wind, where thy boneless arm shall never raise the steel against the lovely.

Long we fought on the heath. The groans of Minvas were lost in the clash of steel. The spear of my foe at last gave way, and he fell before me. The moon looked forth from the skirts of a dark cloud, and I beheld my friend, the brother of Minvas in his blood.

And art thou fallen, my brother, said the faultering voice of the maid; and shall thy father never behold thy return from the chace?—Oh, Moralt! on what distant land does thy spear rise against the mighty?—No brother of mine shall now call thee from the
fields

fields of thy fame. But thou wilt some time return, my hero, and raise the tomb of Minvas near the groves of our former loves.————

I drew the steel from the breast of the lovely. My tears mingled with the red stream from her bosom. She opened her faint eyes, and beheld her Morali's hands bathed in her blood.——She shrieked herself into a ghost. I strove to grasp it in my arms; but it fled with horror from my embrace, and rose on a beam of the moon.

Four stones mark the dwelling of the hero: Near it rose the tomb of the lovely. The virgins often give the tear of pity as they pass: The tenants of the bush sing their songs of woe. All night I sit, and listen to the wind. Dark clouds frown on me as they roll over my head. The children of the air shun me with horror.

What

What faint beam, with its half-formed smile, gladdens the cheek of the east? The moon is asleep in her heathy bed, and the sun is not yet prepared to step forth in the brightness of his beauty.——It is Minvas, the maid of the bloody bosom, coming with her hundred meteors to light Moralt, the hero of other lands, to the fields of death.

In wrath the virgin comes not to her friends. She pursues the gloom of night from our mountains. The morning star trembles in her hand. She comes like the first beam which the sun sends forth to proclaim his approach before he leaves his bed of rest in the east.

Why dost thou fly from us in haste, maid of the mild aspect?——But thou hast left morning on our hills; and thy dim form has disappeared, like a cloud of mist on the lake, which vanishes before the face of the sire of brightness.

Morduth.

F   Crimora

CRIMORA and CONNAL.

Crimora.

Who cometh from the hill, like a cloud tinged with the beam of the west? Whose voice is that, loud as the wind, but pleasant as the harp of Carril? It is my love in the light of steel; but sad is his darkened brow! Live the mighty race of Fingal! or what darkens in Connals soul?

Connal.

They live. They return from the chace, like a stream of light. The sun is on their shields. Like a ridge of fire they descend the hill. Loud is the voice of the youth! The war, my love, is near! To-morrow the dreadful Dargo comes to try the force

of

of our race. The race of Fingal he defies; the race of battle and wounds.

Crimora.

Connal, I saw his sails like grey mist on the dark-brown wave. They slowly came to land. Connal, many are the warriors of Dargo!

Connal.

Bring me thy fathers shield: the bossy, iron shield of Rinval; that shield, like the full=orbed moon, when she moves darkened thro' heaven.

Crimora.

That shield I bring, O Connal; but it did not defend my father. By the spear of Gormar he fell. Thou mayest fall, O Connal.

Connal.

Connal.

Fall I may! But raise my tomb, Crimora!
Grey stones, a mound of earth, shall send my name
to other times. Bend thy red eye over my grave,
beat thy mournful heaving breast. Though fair
thou art my love, as the light; more pleasant than
the gale of the hill; yet I will not here remain.
Raise my tomb, Crimora.

Crimora.

Then give me those arms that gleam; that sword,
and that spear of steel. I shall meet Dargo with
Connal, and aid him in the fight. Farewell, ye
rocks of Ardven! ye deer! and ye streams of the
hill!—We shall return no more. Our tombs
are distant far!

"And did they return no more?" said Utha's
bursting

bursting sigh. " Fell the mighty in battle, and did Crimora live?——Her steps were lonely; her soul was sad for Connal. Was he not young and lovely; like the beam of the setting sun?" Ullin saw the virgins tear, he took the softly trembling harp: the song was lovely, but sad, and silence was in Carric=thura.

Autumn is dark on the mountains; grey mists rests on the hills. The whirlwind is heard on the heath. Dark rolls the river through the narrow plain. A tree stands alone on the hill, and marks the slumbering Connal. The leaves whirl round with the wind, and strew the grave of the dead. At times are seen here the ghosts of the departed, when the musing hunter alone, stalks slowly over the heath.

Who can reach the source of thy race, O Connal? Who recount thy fathers? Thy family grew like an

oak

oak on the mountain, but now it is torn from the earth. Who shall supply the place of Connal? Here was the din of arms; here the groans of the dying. Bloody are the wars of Fingal! O Connal! it was here thou didst fall. Thine arm was like a storm; thy sword a beam of the sky; thy height a rock on the plain; thine eyes, a furnace of fire. Louder than a storm was thy voice, in the battles of thy steel. Warriors fell by thy sword, as the thistle by the staff of a boy. Dargo the mighty came on, darkening in his rage. His brows were gathered into wrath. His eyes like two caves in a rock. Bright rose their swords on each side; loud was the clang of their steel.

The daughter of Rinval was near; Crimora bright in the armour of man; her yellow hair is loose behind, her bow is in her hand. She followed the
youth

youth to the war, Connal her much beloved. She drew the string on Dargo; but erring she pierced her Connal. He falls like an oak on the plain; like a rock from the shaggy hill. What shall she do, haplefs maid!——He bleeds, her Connal dies! All the night long she cries, and all the day, "O Connal, my love and my friend! With grief the sad mourner dies! Earth here incloses the lovelicst pair on the hill. The grafs grows between the stones of their tomb; I often sit in the mournful shade. The wind sighs through the grafs; their memory rushes on my mind. Undisturbed you now sleep together; in the tomb of the mountain you rest alone! And soft be their rest, said Utha, haplefs children of streamy Lutha! I will remember them with tears, and my secret song shall rise; when the winds of the north bends the proud groves of Tora.

Carric-thura.

The

The PRAISE of CARTHON.

Fingal was sad for Carthon; he commanded his bards to mark the day when shadowy autumn returned: and often did they mark the day, and sing the hero's praise. "Who comes so dark from ocean's roar, like autumn's shadowy cloud? Death is trembling in his hand! his eyes are flames of fire!——Who roars along dark Lora's heath? Who but Carthon, king of swords? The people fall! See! how he strides, like the sullen ghost of Morven!—— But there he lies, a goodly oak, which sudden blasts overturned! When shall thou rise, Balclutha's joy. When Carthon shalt thou arise?——Who comes, so dark from ocean's roar, like autumn's shadowy cloud?" Such were the words of the bards, in the day of their

mourning

mourning: Ossian often joined their voice; and added to their song. My soul has been mournful for Carthon; he fell in the days of his youth: And thou, O Clefsammor! where is thy dwelling in the wind? Has the youth forgot his wound? Flies he on clouds with thee? I feel the sun, O Malvina, leave me to my rest. Perhaps they may come to my dreams; I think I hear a feeble voice!——The beam of heaven delights to shine on the grave of Carthon: I feel it warm around.

O thou that roll'est above, round as the shield of my fathers! Whence are thy beams, O sun! thy everlasting light? thou comest forth in thy awful beauty; the stars hide themselves in the sky; the moon cold and pale, sinks in the western wave. But thou thyself movest alone: who can be a companion of thy course! The oaks of the mountains fall: the

G

mountains

mountains themselves decay with years; the ocean shrinks and grows again: the moon herself is lost in heaven; but thou art for ever the same; rejoicing in the brightness of thy course. When the world is dark with tempests; when the thunder rolls, and lightning flies; thou lookest in thy beauty, from the clouds, and laughest at the storm. But to Ossian, thou lookest in vain; for he beholds thy beams no more; whither thy yellow hair is flown on the eastern clouds, or thou tremblest at the gates of the west. But thou art perhaps like me, for a season, thy years will have an end. Thou shalt sleep in thy clouds, careless of the voice of the morning. Exult then, O sun, in the strength of thy youth! age is dark and unlovely; it is like the glimmering light of the moon, when it shines through broken clouds, and the mist is on the hills.

Carthon.

The

The TALE of the BARD.

Turloch lived at Lubar of streams. In deeds of fame his hair grew white. Strangers knew the way to his hall: In the broad path there grew no mountain grass. No door had he to his gate. 'Why' he said should the wanderer see it shut?——Turloch was tall as the oak of his vale. On either side, a fair branch lifted its green growing head. Two green trees smiling in the shower, and looking thro' rainbows on the sun, were the two children of Turloch. Heroes admired the beauty of Abigul; and virgins, with secret pleasure, beheld the steps of Aithos. 'He is stately,' said the strangers, 'as the son of Turloch, and she is fair,' they said 'as the maid at Lubar's rolling waters.

G 2

Long

Long did the years of Turloch glide smoothly by. Their steps were silent as the stream of his vale. Joy smiled in the face of the chief, like the sun beams on the brow of his hill, when no cloud travels in the road of heaven.

" But ever varying, as the face of the sky, are the days of man upon his mountains. The storm and the calm roll there in their course; the light and the shade by turns are there.

" Migul one day went forth to the chace. In her white hand was the bended bow; and two gray dogs bounded, through the morning dew, in her steps. Swift as mists that fly through heaven when the winds are high, they pursued on hills the deer. Migul drew the string. Her winged darts were unerring as death. On the brown heath the sons of the mountain, gasping, fell.——

" The

" The huntress sits on her rock.   The thunder is heard on the hill.   The clouds gather like night. The streams descending from the mountains are white and Lubar rolls in foam.   How shalt thou cross it to thy home, thou trembling maid?

" Althos saw his sister approach.   He knew where two bending rocks almost met above the stream. An aged oak spreads its arm across: often had the trembling hunters of other times crept along its moss in the day of storm.   Here stood Althos above the deep. ' Give me, my sister, thy hand.'—Both shake upon the bending branch: it quakes; it cracks; it breaks; it falls !

" Turloch was kindling the fire in his hall. My daughter from the hill, he said, is wet.

" A cry strikes his ear, as he fans the flame. Sudden=starting, he faces forth.   He sees his two
children

children shoot along the stream; they are clung to one aged branch.

" He cried; but his cries were vain. Night, descending on the vale was dark. The rocks till morning heard his moan; and deer, awaking at the sound, leapt wildly from Lubar's banks.——Day found him wandering there; and night again overtook him in the same place. But his children at the dark stream he found not; and sad he returned to his empty house. Long did it echo to his sighs; and long did he wander at the dark stream, when the children of the vale had retired to rest.

" The shield of battle, at length, was struck. Turloch heard, as he wept on Lubar's banks, the sound. He sailed with his people to Jalin; but they landed, as they passed, in Ithulmo.——There, two lovely beams met them on the rock; benders of
the

the bow, when bounds before them the dun roe. The eye of Turloch darkened with grief as he beheld their beauty, in the midst of the children of the isle.——
‘ Two such lovely beams were you once in my sight, my children! Such was thy stateliness, O Althos! and such thy beauty, O Migul!’

" They heard the voice of their father, on the isle to which they were borne, by the oak, on the wing of streams. They heard it and sprang to his arms with joy.——The face of the aged again was bright; and gladness returned to Lubar."

" Thy children, O Alurno," added the voice of age, " are, like those of Turloch, only lost for a season. They are only gone before thee on their own stream to the land of the happy. There thou shalt soon behold them lovely, lifting their young heads in the midst of heroes. Already, their course is in the fair

mists

mists that wander on the face of the moon; when she
looks pale through clouds, and shines in the stream of
Alva.   Let, therefore, the grief of Uran be forgot,
for there he will find his Lorma.   Let the tear of
the red eye of Murno be wiped off for there he will
find his children."

The grief of the mourners calmed by degrees. Uran
was like a tree, which though the storm is laid, still
shakes its waving head; and the bosom of Murno still
heaved above the sigh; like waves which tofs themselves,
at times, after the winds have retired.

Lamentation

LAMENTATION of MURNO.

"Morning rose on the isle of Croma, and the horn of my son was heard. Three gray dogs leap around him and lift their ears with joy at the sound of his quiver. They bound in their skiff through the strait, and pursue the dark-brown deer of Croma. With evening we see the skiff return. The waves arise on the deep. The skiff is seen at times on their white tops: but suddenly sinking it disappears. In vain we look for it again; it is concealed in the sea, or in night.

"My soul trembled for my son.—But old as I was, what could I do?—I bade the years that were past return; but they heard me not.—The path of their course was distant, and the voice of

H   Murno

Murno was feeble. My daughter too shrieked, and shook my aged soul, as shakes the blast the dry leaf of the desart.——' O my brother! my brother! of love! in the storm art thou lost? Art thou lost my brother?'

" Dim appears a dark spot on the foamy top of a wave.——Is that the wandering ooze; or is it thou my brother?'——He heard her voice; and with one faint note he replied. Fear and joy divide, by turns her soul.——Two of the gray dogs had reached the shore, the third, in the foam of the waves was lost. The two heard the voice of Finan fail. They bound again into the surgy deep. They return with Finan on the third wave; but one breathes on the beach his last.

" Lorma bore her brother to the rock. ' Here,'

he

he faintly said, ' Let me for a little, rest, for my strength is failed.'

" She wrapt her robe about his breast, and made his pillow of the reeds that were driest.

" He sleeps. The maid in silence bends over his face. She bids the waves be still, and the noisy path of their whales be distant. And distant be your rustling course, ye winds of the mountain; and soft be your gliding, ye stream from the vale of hinds. Quiet, through the bosom of the woods, be the noise of your torrents; and silent through rustling leaves, be your steps ye dun-bounding roes, Let my brother of love sleep, for his eyes are heavy. Soft, Finan, on the dark rock be thy sleep, calm my brother of love be thy slumbers.

" But, ah me! his face is pale; it is wan, as the moon in her gray watry cloud. The

H 2

countenance

countenance of my brother is unlovely. Perhaps he still dreams of the troubled deep; for his brow is dark. It is clouded as the face of children in their unsettled rest, when their dreams are of the coming of wolves. Mothers of the tender soul, do you then awake your children from their slumbers? Do you bid their sleep depart, and scatter, as mist on the gale, the fear of their dreams? Yes, you do awake them: but I will not awake my brother of love till the morning come, for his strength is failed; his sleep is heavy.——But the flies of night disturb thee Finan. How shall I keep them away? Thy face with my own I will softly cover; but I will not dispel thy slumber.——Ah! my brother, thou art cold.——Thou hast no breath——Thou art dead! my brother! O my brother!——

" Her cries ascend on the rock. As I approach
they

they strike my ear. The sea grows, and she perceives it not. She loads with her cries the wind. The beating on her white breast is loud; the howling of the gray dog is wild. My soul melts on the shore with grief. Often it bade me rush to the relief of my child. But the voice within me said, ' Murno, thou art old and feeble; the days of thy cleaving the deep are over.'

" The gathering wave lifts my children from the rock: it tosses them on its breast to the shore. There dark rocks meet them with their force, and the side of Lorma is torn. Her blood tinge the wave: her soul is on the same blast with Finan.

" Sad O my children have you left your father: the name of parent I will hear no more. I stand on the heath, a blasted oak; no more shall my branches flourish. Autumn is on the plain. The trees are
bare

bare on the brown heath. Their leaves with the spring shall return; but no green leaf of mine shall lift in the summer shower, its head. The race of Alva is failed, like the blue smoke of its halls when the beam of the oak is decayed.——Great is the cause of Murno's grief; for one night hath seen him without a child. Thy tomb O Finan is here; and here thy grave, O Lorma!"——

——The soul of the aged was sad. The burst of his grief still arose: we remain silent in our place, like ghosts when the winds are calm; like a stream of ice, when it sleeps between two banks of snow, and shews to the pale moon its glittering beard.

——But who comes, wandering, wild on the mountains, like the roe that hath lost his companion among the woody streams. His yellow hair wanders on the dark breath of winds. Unequal are his steps.

Frequent

Frequent the burst of his grief: the sigh of his breast is mournful. It is like the voice of a blast in a cave, when the waves, before it, toss themselves in a storm. It is Uran the bender of the bow; the love of thy youth, O Lorma! He had come to Dunalva in the night of storms: but the halls were silent and dark. Two blue stars had used to shine there. But now he saw them not; set were the eyes of Lorma.

" Lorma, where dost thou rest? My love where are thy slumbers? Has the night seized thee in the lonely chace; has darkness hid thy steps in the desart? Daughter of the bow, where dost thou rest? O that I knew thy place; then should I haste to find thee! Dost thou sleep at the foot of a gray rock; is thy bed of moss on the bank of streams? Ah me! if it is, the breasts of my love will be wet: they will be wet, and the night is cold.——It is cold: but peaceful be thy

rest

rest, dweller of the soul of Uran; let thy dreams of me be lovely.——

——"Disturb her not, ye spirits of the night on your blasts; ruffle not her hair, ye winds, blow not away that smile on the lips of my love.——My love is calm in the midst of storms; for the thoughts of her soul in the season of rest is Uran.——Glide smoothly by her, ye streams of the valley of roes: skip quietly ye dun sons of the mountain, through your bush. Eagles of the hill of hinds, let the rustling of your wings, in the desart, be distant. See that ye disturb not the dreams of my love; that ye awake not the slumbers of Lorma.——Sleep on, O Lorma; let not the murmur of the stream, nor the rustling of the storm in trees, affright thee. Sleep on; with the morning I will come and awake thee. I will awake thee, but my voice will be soft. It will rise in thy

ear

ear like the hum of the mountain bee, when he travels on the wing of the breeze at a distance. The voice is lost at times: the brown son of the wing is drinking the dew of roses, where they grow on their secret banks.——Sleep on, O Lorma; and if the slumber of night descends on the soul of Uran, rise thou in the dream of his rest, and let the look of thy eye be lovely. He rested on the mossy bank. Sleep half descended on his soul. The murmur of Alva in his ear was less. The moon still looked through the windows of his rest;——before him twice arose the sighing Lorma. She was like a white cloud before the moon, when her light is dim, and her countenance sad. Uran knew the ghost of his love. He wandered, mournful, wild on the heath. The voice of Murno reached his ear: he perceived two green mounds of earth. He dropped his bow. He

I

fell.

fell. But why should I tell the grief of Uran? Silence was long on the hill. The bard of Morven, at length, took the harp.——We leaned forward our breasts upon its sound, and listened as he sung with the voice of grief.

Finan and Lorma.

The

The BROTHERS.

I-Thorno, that risest midst ridgy seas! Why is thy head so gloomy, in the oceans mist? From thy vales come forth a race, fearless as thy strong-winged eagles; the race of Colgorm of iron shields, dwellers of Loda's hall.

In Tormuth's resounding isle, arose Lurthan, streamy hill. It bent its woody head high over a silent vale. There at foamy Cruruth's source, dwelt Rurmar, hunter of boars! His daughter was fair as a sun-beam, white-bosomed Strina-dona.

Many a king of heroes, and hero of iron shields; many a youth of heavy locks came to Rurmar's echoing hall. They came to woo the maid, the stately huntress

of

of Tormuth wild; but thou lookest careless from thy steps, high-bosomed Strina-dona!

——If on the heath she moved, her breast was whiter than the down of Cana; if on the sea beat shore, than the foam of the rolling ocean. Her eyes were two stars of light. Her face was heavens bow in showers. Her dark hair flowed round it, like the streaming clouds, thou wert the dweller of souls, white-handed Strina-dona.

Colgorm came in his ship, and Corcul-Suran, king of shells. The Brothers came from I-Thorno, to woo the sun-beam of Tormuth wild. She saw them in their echoing steel. Her soul was fixed on blue-eyed Colgorm. Ul-lochlin's nightly eye looked in, and saw the tossing arms of Strina-dona.

——Wrathful the brothers frowned. Their flaming eyes, in silence, met. They turned away.
They

They struck their shields. Their hands were trembling on their swords. They rushed into the strife of heroes, for, long-haired Strina-dona.

Corcul-Suran fell in blood. On his isle, raged the strength of his father. He turned Colgorm, from I-Thorno, to wander on all the winds. In Crathmo-craulo's rocky field, he dwelt by a foreign stream. Nor darkened the king alone, that beam of light was near, the daughter of echoing Tormuth, white-armed Strina-dona.

Cathloda.

Vinvela

DINDCIN and SHILRIC.

Dinvela.

My love is of the hill. He pursues the flying deer: his grey dogs are panting around him; his bowstring sounds in the wind. Dost thou rest by the fount of the rock, or by the noise of the mountain stream? The rushes are nodding to the wind, the mist flies over the hill. I will approach my love unseen; I will behold him from the rock. Lovely I saw thee first by the aged oak of Branno; thou wert returning tall from the chace; the fairest among thy friends.

Shilric.

What voice is that I hear? that voice like the

summer

summer wind! I sit not by the nodding rushes; I hear not the fount of the rock. Afar, Vinvela, afar I go to the wars of Fingal. My dogs attend me no more. No more I tread the hill. No more from on high I see thee, fair moving by the stream of the plain; bright as the bow of heaven; as the moon on the western wave.

Vinvela.

Then thou art gone, O Shilric! I am alone on the hill! the deer are seen on the brow; void of fear they graze along. No more they dread the wind; no more the rustling tree. The hunter is far removed; he is in the field of graves. Strangers? sons of the waves! Spare my lovely Shilric!

Shilric.

If fall I must in the field, raise high my grave,
Vinvela.

Vinvela. Grey stones and heaped up earth, shall mark me to future times. When the hunter shall sit by the mound, and produce his food at noon, " some warrior rests here," he will say; and my fame shall live in his praise. Remember me Vinvela, when low on earth I lie.

Vinvela.

Yes! I will remember thee; alas! my Shilric will fall! what shall I do, my love! When thou art for ever gone? Through these hills I will go at noon: I will go through the silent heath. There I will see the place of thy rest, returning from the chace. Alas! my Shilric will fall; but I will remember Shilric.——

——And I remember the chief said the king of woody Morven; he consumed the battle in his

rage

rage. But now my eyes behold him not. I met him, one day, on the hill; his cheek was pale; his brow was dark. The sigh was frequent in his breast: his steps were towards the desart. But now he is not in the croud of my chiefs, when the sound of my shields arise. Dwells he in the narrow house, the chief of high Cormora?

Cronnan, said Ullin of other times, raise the song of Shilric; when he returned to his hills, and Vinvela was no more. He leaned on her grey mofsy stone; he thought Vinvela lived. He saw her fair moving on the plain: but the bright form lasted not: the sun-beam fled from the field, and she was seen no more. Hear the song of Shilric; it is soft but sad!——

I sit by the mofsy fountain; on the top of the hill of winds. One tree is rustling above me.

K   Dark

Dark waves roll over the heath. The lake is troubled below. The deer descend from the hill.——No hunter at a distance is seen. It is mid=day. but all is silent. Sad are my thoughts alone. Didst thou but appear, O my love, a wanderer on the heath! Thy hair floating on the wind behind thee: thy bosom heaving on the sight: thine eyes full of tears for thy friends, whom the mist of the hill had concealed! Thee, I would comfort my love, and bring thee to thy fathers house!

But is it she that there appears, like a beam of light on the heath! bright as the moon in autumn, as the sun in a summer storm, comest thou, O maid, over rocks, over mountains, to me? She speaks; but how weak her voice! like the breeze in the reeds of the lake.

"Returnest thou safe from the war? Where are
thy

thy friends, my love? I heard and mourned thee, Shilric! Yes, my fair, I return; but I alone of my race. Thou shalt see them no more: Their graves I raised on the plain. But why art thou on the desert hill? Why on the heath alone.?"

Alone I am, O Shilric! alone in the winter house. With grief, for thee I fell. Shilric, I am pale in the tomb. She fleets, she sails away; as mist before the wind! and, wilt thou not stay, Vinvela? Stay and behold my tears! fair thou appearest, Vinvela, fair thou wast, when alive!

By the mossy fountain I will sit; on the top of the hill of winds. When mid=day is silent around, O talk with me, Vinvela! come on the light=winged gale! on the breeze of the desart come! let me hear thy voice, as thou passest, when mid=day is silent around!

Carricthura.

Death

DEATH of CULALIN.

Graceful on the hills was Culalin, the maid of the hand of snow. Her dark hair rose on the wind like the raven's wing. The heaving of her white breast was as the downy bosom of the swan, when the soft waves meet it in gladneſs. The beauty of each virgin vanished when the daughter of Sonner appeared. Graceful was the mother of my sons, and gladneſs shone in my hall when her soft voice joined the harp.

Guigan, the daughter of Ainer, had tasted my secret embrace before I saw Culalin, and she turned the red eye of envy on the pride of women. She came to Culalin in the season of her solitude, and spoke the words of deceit.

Pleasant are the smiles of the mid-day sun, Culalin!

Culalin! cool the shade beneath the birchen boughs.
The hunters are distant far. The sea has borne her
waves to other lands, and left our rocks to raise their
dark heads before the kindly breeze. Come, daughter
of Sonner, and taste the sweets of noon.

They wandered through the forest. A tall rock
within the verge of ocean's bed, affords a grateful
shade. Sleep shut the eyes of Culalin. Guigan
plet her long hair with thongs, and fixed them to
the cliffy rock. Her hands of snow are bound:
her feet are tied to a stone. The maid of the
gloomy soul saw the coming of the flood. She
rejoiced in the blackness of her deeds, and fled.

Ocean came with all his tumbling waves, Culalin
startled at the sound.——Where art thou, my friend?
Save me, Guigan, from the hostile flood.——
The rocks answered in pity to her groans: sighs
issued

issued from each hollow cave. But soon shall ye cease to mourn for my love, ye sons of the rock! Another wave, and she lies peaceful beneath the stream. The retiring flood shall leave her as food for the ravenous children of the sea.

The strength of thy brother's arm, Guigan, though he was my best, my dearest friend, was no shield to thee. Alas! the hero fell before my sword. He who saved my life in battle, died by my hand. Thou also sleepest near him, cruel maid, and thy ghost often frowns on me in the season of dreams.

But thou, Culalin, of the raven locks! pleasant art thou in thy loveliness, as thou smilest on the couch of thy slumbers. No surly looks are thine. No traveller shuns thy dwelling in the season of noon. Often didst thou raise thy shrill voice on thy rocks, and warn the mariner of the coming storm. He hears
the

the unerring sound, and retires within the peaceful bosom of the creek. In safety he views the conflict of the waves, and blesses the friendly sound of thy rocks, thou watcher of the nightly storms!

Thus have I slain my friend, Morralt; yet my spear rises with success against the foe.——The lovely rise but to fall: the mighty gather strength but to sink.

——Silent and gloomy sat the listening host. Sighs broke forth at the close of the tale of woe. The forest ceased to wave its dark head: the short-limbed heath stood still. Clouds were fixed in the face of heaven. No rocks contended with the blast. Peace was proclaimed among the vegetable race; for the wind ceased to travel.

Morduth.

Comal

COMAL and GALBINA.

Comal was a son of Albin; the chief of an hundred hills! his deer drank of a thousand streams. A thousand rocks replied to the voice of his dogs. His face was the mildness of youth. His hand, the death of heroes. One was his love, and fair was she! the daughter of mighty Conloch. She appeared like a sun-beam among women. Her dogs were taught to the chace. Her bowstring sounded on the winds. Her soul was fixed on Comal. Often met their eyes of love. Their course in the chace was one. Happy were their words in secret. But Grumal loved the maid, the dark chief of gloomy Ardven. He watched her lone steps on the heath; the foe of unhappy Comal.

—One

—One day, tired of the chace, when the mist had concealed their friends, Comal and the daughter of Conloch met, in the cave of Ronan. It was the wonted haunt of Comal. The sides were hung with his arms. A hundred shields of thongs were there; a hundred helms of sounding steel. "Rest here," he said my love Galbina: thou light of the cave of Ronan! a deer appears on Mora's brow. I go; but I will soon return." "I fear," she said, " dark Grumal my foe: he haunts the cave of Ronan! I will rest among the arms, but soon return my love!"

He went to the deer of Mora. The daughter of Conloch would try his love. She cloathed her fair sides with his armour; she strode from the cave of Ronan! he thought it was his foe. His heart beat high. His colour changed, and darkness dimmed his eyes. He drew the bow. The arrow

L

flew.

flew. Galbina fell in blood! he ran with wildnefs in his steps: he called the daughter of Conloch. No answer in the lonely rock. Where art thou, O my love? He saw, at length, her heaving heart, beating around the arrow he threw. " O Conloch's daughter, is it thou? he sunk upon her breast! The hunters found the haplefs pair; he afterwards walked the hill. But many and silent were his steps around the dark dwelling of his love. The fleet of the ocean came. He fought, the strangers fled. He searched for death along the field. But who could slay the mighty Comal! he threw away his dark=brown shield. An arrow found his manly breast. He sleeps with his loved Galbina, at the noise of the sounding surge! Their green tombs are seen by the mariner, when he bounds on the waves of the north.

Fingal.

Fainasollis

FAINASOLLIS.

"Oscar! I was young like thee, when lovely
Fainasollis came: that sun-beam, that mild light of
love! The daughter of Craca's king! I then returned
from Cona's heath, and few were in my train. A
white-sailed boat appeared afar off; we saw it like a
mist, that rode on ocean's wind. It soon approached.
We saw the fair. Her white breast heaved with sighs.
The wind was in her dark hair: her rosy cheek had
tears. "Daughter of beauty," calm I said, "what
sigh is in thy breast? Can I, young as I am defend
thee, daughter of the sea? My sword is not
unmatched in war, but dauntless is my heart,"

"To thee I fly," with sighs she said, "O prince
of mighty men! To thee I fly, chief of the generous

L 2

shells,

shells, supporter of the feeble hand! The king of Craca's echoing isle owned me the sun-beam of his race. Cromala's halls have heard the sighs of love, for unhappy Tainasollis! Sora's chief beheld me fair; he loved the daughter of Craca. His sword is a beam of light upon the warriors side. But dark is his brow; and tempests are in his soul. I shun him, on the roaring sea; but Sora's chief pursues?"

"Rest thou," I said, "behind my shield; rest in peace, thou beam of light! The gloomy chief of Sora will fly, if Fingal's arm is like his soul. In some lone cave I might conceal thee, daughter of the sea! But Fingal never flies. Where the danger threatens, I rejoice in the storm of spears." I saw the tears upon her check. I pitied Craca's fair. Now, like a dreadful wave afar, appeared the ship of

stormy

stormy Borbar. His masts high-bended over the sea, behind their sheets of snow. White roll the waves on either side. The strength of ocean sounds. "Come thou," I said, "from the roar of ocean, thou rider of the storm! Partake of the feast within my hall. It is the house of strangers."

The maid stood trembling by my side. He drew the bow. She fell. "Unerring is thy hand," I said, "but feeble was the foe!" We fought, nor weak the strife of death! He sunk beneath my sword. We laid them in two tombs of stone; the hapless lovers of youth! Such have I been in my youth, O Oscar; be thou like the age of Fingal. Never search thou for battle; nor shun it when it comes.——

Fingal.

Address

ADDRESS to the MOON.

Daughter of heaven fair art thou! the silence of thy face is pleasant! thou comest forth in thy loveliness. The stars attend thy blue course in the east. The clouds rejoice in thy presence, O moon: they brighten their dark-brown sides. Who is like thee in heaven, light of the silent night? the stars are ashamed in thy presence. They turn away their sparkling eyes. Whither dost thou retire from thy course, when the darkness of thy countenance grows? hast thou thy hall like Ossian? dwellest thou in the shadow of grief? have thy sisters fallen from heaven? are they who rejoiced with thee, at night, no more? Yes! they are fallen, fair light! and thou dost often retire to mourn. But thou, thyself shalt fail, one night;

and

and leave thy blue path in heaven. The stars will then lift their heads: they, who were ashamed in thy presence, will rejoice. Thou art now clothed with thy brightness. Look from thy gates in the sky. Burst the cloud, O wind, that the daughter of night may look forth; that the shaggy mountains may brighten, and the ocean roll its white waves in light.——

Dartbula.

Moina.

MOINA.

" Moina fell in Balclutha, for I have seen her ghost. I knew her as she came through the dusky night, along the murmur of Lora: she was like the new moon, seen through the gathered mist: when the sky pours down its flaky snow, and the world is silent and dark."

" Raise ye bards, said the mighty Fingal, the praise of unhappy Moina. Call her ghost, with your songs, to our hills; that she may rest with the fair of Morven, the sun=beams of other days, the delights of heroes of old. I have seen the walls of Balclutha, but they were desolate. The fire had resounded in the halls: and the voice of the people is heard no more. The stream of Clutha was

removed

removed from its place, by the fall of the walls The thistle shook, there its lonely head: the moss whistled to the wind, the fox looked out from the windows, the rank grass of the wall waved round its head. Desolate is the dwelling of Moina, silence is in the house of her fathers. Raise the song of mourning, O bards, over the land of strangers. They have but fallen before us: for one day we must fall. Why dost thou build the hall, son of the winged days? Thou lookest from thy towers to day; yet a few years, and the blast of the desart comes; it howls in thy empty court, and whistles round thy half=worn shield! and let the blast of the desart come: we shall be renowned in our day! the mark of my arm shall be in battle; my name in the song of bards. Raise the song; send round the shell: let joy be heard in my hall.

Carthon.

M

Lamentation

LAMENTATION of MINONA.

The spouse of Dargo came in tears: for Dargo was no more! The heroes sigh over Lartho's Chief: and what shall sad Mingala do? The dark soul vanished like morning mist, before the king of spears: but the generous glowed in his presence like the morning star.

Who was the fairest and most lovely? Who but Collath's stately son? Who sat in the midst of the wise, but Dargo of the mighty deeds?

Thy hand touched the trembling harp: thy voice was soft as summer-winds. Ah me! what shall the heroes say? for Dargo fell before a boar. Pale is the lovely cheek; the look of which was firm in

danger!

danger! why hast thou failed on our hills, thou fairer than the beams of the sun?

The daughter of Adonfrin was lovely in the eyes of the valiant; she was lovely in their eyes, but she chose to be the spouse of Dargo.

But thou art alone, Mingala! the night is coming with its clouds; where is the bed of thy repose? where but in the tomb of Dargo?

Why dost thou lift the stone O bard! why dost thou shut the narrow house? Mingala's eyes are heavy, bard! she must sleep with Dargo.

Last night I heard the song of joy in Lartho's lofty hall. But silence dwells around my bed.——Mingala rests with Dargo.——

Dargo.

M 2

Death

DEATH OF DAR-THULA.

Dar-thula stood in silent grief! No tear is in her eye, but her look is wildly sad. Pale was her cheek. Her trembling lips broke short an half-formed word. Her dark hair flew on the wind. The gloomy Cairbar came, " where is thy lover now? The car-borne chief of Etha? hast thou beheld the halls of Usnoth? or the dark-brown hills of Fingal? My battle would have roared on Morven, had not the winds met Dar-thula. Fingal himself would have been low, and sorrow dwelling in Selma!" Her shield fell from Dar-thula's arm. Her breast of snow appeared. It appeared; but it was stained with blood. An arrow was fixed in her side. She

fell

fell on her fallen lover like a wreath of snow! Her hair spreads wildly on his face. Their blood is mixing around!"

"Daughter of Colla! thou art low!" said Cairbar's hundred bards. " Silence is at the blue streams of Selma. Truthil's race have failed. When wilt thou rise in thy beauty, first of Erin's maids? Thy sleep is long in the tomb. The morning distant far. The sun shall not come to thy bed and say, " awake Dar-thula! awake thou first of women! The wind of spring is abroad! the flowers shake their heads on the green hills. The woods wave their growing leaves. Retire, O sun, the daughter of Colla is asleep. She will not come forth in her beauty. She will not move in the steps of her loveliness."

Fingal.

The

The Lamentation of FINGAL over GAUL.

Who can tell the sadness of Morven's heroes? They come in silence, each from his own winding vale; slowly moving, like the shadow of mist on the brown rushy plain, when the wind is scarce awake on the hill. They see the bulwark of the battle low; and their bursting tears, like the ooze of rocks, descend. Fingal leaned to the blasted pine, that was overturned at the head of Gaul. His gray locks, as he bends, half hide his tears; but in his white beard they meet the whistling wind.——

"And art thou fallen," at length he said: "art thou fallen first of my heroes! Shall I hear thy voice no more in my halls, nor the sound of thy shield in my battles? Shall thy sword no more lighten
the

the dark path of my danger; nor thy spear scatter whole hosts of my enemies? Shall thy dark ship ride no more the storm, while thy joyful rovers pour before them the song on the watry mountains? Shall the children of Morven no more awake my soul from its thought as they cry, 'behold the ship of Gaul!' Shall the harps of virgins and the voice of bards, no more be heard when thou art coming?——I see not the red=streams of thy banners on the heath; the tread of thy foot is not there; nor the sound of thy unmissing arrow. The bounding of thy dogs is not on the hill; they mournfully howl in the door of thy empty house. The deer grazes on the plain before them: but they weep on; they do not heed him; for they see not Gaul returning.——Alas! sons of the chace, the day of his return is past. His glad voice shall call you no more, in the morning, to

pursue

pursue the steps of roes thro' rocky mountains.——Here
forgetful of the chace, he rests; nor can even the
sound of Morven's shield, O Gaul, awake thee!

"Strength of the warrior, what art thou? To
day, thou rollest the battle, a cloud of dust, before
thee; and the dead strew thy path, as the withered
leaves mark the course of a ghost of night.——To
morrow, the short dream of thy valour is over; the
terror of thousands is vanished. The beetle, on his
dusky wing, hums the song of triumph over the mighty;
and unmolested offends him.——

"Why son of the feeble, didst thou wish for the
strength of the chief of Strumon, when thou didst
behold him brightening in the course of his steel, as
brightens a pillar of ice in the midst of sun=beams?
didst thou not know that the strength of the warrior
soon fails, as melts in the beam that ice which thou
hast

hast been viewing? Its date is short; like the bright cloud that glitters to the ray of the evening. The hunter sees it from his rock, as he hies from home, and admires the rainbow form of its beauty. But a few moments, on their eagle pinions, pass, the sun shuts his eye of light; the blast whirls that way his rustling course, and a dark mist is all that remains of the gay form.——It is all O Gaul! that now remains of thee.——But thy memory chief of Fingal's heroes, shall remain, no cloud of mist, that shall pass away, on its own gray mist is thy fame.

Raise, ye bards his tomb; with that of the sun beam of his love, Evirchoma.——This gray stone shall mark to the traveller the place of his repose; and that tall oak shall shade it from the noon day heat. The passing breeze shall bid its boughs be early green, and long preserve their beauty. Its leaves shall

N

shoot

shoot out their head, through the flower of the spring, while other trees are still bare, and the heath around them blasted. The birds of summer, from their distant land, shall first perch on Strumon's oak; from afar they shall behold its green beauty. The ghost of Gaul will hear, in his cloud, their song; and the virgins of the race to come will praise Evirchoma. The memory of you two, while these monuments remain, shall travel thro' future years together.——Then when thou, O stone, shalt crumble into dust; and thou O tree, moulder with age away; when thou, mighty stream, shalt cease to run, and the mountain=spring shall, no more supply thy course; when your songs, O bards, in the dark flood of time shall be lost; and the memory of yourselves, with these you sung, in its vast current be swept away and forgot.——

Gaul.

The

DEATH of DERMID.

Dermid falls like a tall pine on the heath, how quick the colour forsakes his cheek.——It was red as the fruit that bends the mountain tree; but now is grown pale as the withered grass. A dark cloud spreads over his countenance, as thick mists that veil the face of the wintery sun, when the evening comes before its time.——

"The shades of night gather on my eyes. I feel the decay of my strength. The tide that flowed in my heart has ebbed away. Behind it I remain, a cold unmoving rock.——Thou shalt know it, Guaina, and be sad; ah! the pain of death is to part with my love.——But the shades of the night are gathering over my soul. Let Dermid sleep; his eyes are heavy."

Wh

Who shall tell it to Graina?——But she is nigh. She leans beneath the shade of a tree. She hears the moans of her love, they awake her slumbering soul. Hark! she pours her faint song on the calm breath of the breeze. See! her blood and her tears wander on her white breasts, like dark streams on the mountains of snow.

"My love is fallen! O place me in his bed of earth, at the foot of that rock, which lifts through aged trees its ivy head. The sheeted stream, with murmuring grief, shall throw its waters over our tomb; but O! let it not wet the dark-brown hair of my love. The stream still murmurs by; some day its course may wash away the mound. The hunter, as whistling he goes careless by, will perceive the bow of Dermid, and say, 'This is Dermid's grave.' His spouse perhaps may be with him. Near the bow she will observe
this

this arrow in my breast; and say as she wipes her eye,
' Here was Graina laid beside her love.'——Musing
they move silently along; their thoughts are of the
narrow house. They look on each other, through
glistening eyes. ' The fondest lovers,' say they,
' must part at last.'

" But stop hunters of the mountain, and give the
mighty his praise. No mean hunter of a little vale
was he, whom you have passed so careless by.——His
fame was great among the heroes of Morven; his arm
was strong in their battles: and why should I speak
of his beauty; shall his comeliness remain with him
in the tomb!——His breast was as the down of the
mountains, or the snow on the tree of the vale, when
it waves its head in the sun.——Red was the cheek,
and blue the eye, of my love.——Like the grass of
the rock, slow-bending in the breeze, were his brows;

and

and sweeter than the music of harps, or the songs of of the groves, was thy voice to virgins, O Dermid! But the music of thy voice is ceased, and my spirits can no more be cheered. The burden of my grief is heavy: the songs of Morven's bards cannot remove it. It will not listen to all the larks that soar in the lonly vale, when the deny plains rejoice in the morning sun of Summer.——But what hath Graina to do with the sun of the morning; or what hath Dermid to do with summer? when shall the sun rise in the tomb? when shall it be summer in the grave, or morning in the narrow house? Never shall that morning shine, that shall dispel our slumber, O Dermid.

Dermid.

Song

SONG of MALVINA.

"It was the voice of my love! seldom art thou, in the dreams of Malvina! open your airy halls, O fathers of Toscar of shields! unfold the gates of your clouds: the steps of Malvina are near. I have heard a voice in my dream. I feel the fluttering of my soul. "Why didst thou come, O blast, from the dark-rolling face of the lake? thy rustling wing was in the tree; the dream of Malvina fled. But she beheld her love, when his robe of mist flew on the wind. A sun-beam was on his skirts, they glittered like the gold of the stranger. It was the voice of my love! seldom comes he to my dreams!"

"But thou dwellest in the soul of Malvina, son of mighty Ossian! My sighs arise with the beam of

the

the east; my tears descend with the drops of night. I was a lone tree, in thy presence, Oscar, with all my branches round me, but thy death came like a blast from the desart, and laid my green head low. The spring returned with its showers; no leaf of mine arose! The virgins saw me silent in the hall; they touched the harp of joy. The tear was on the cheek of Malvina: the virgins beheld me in my grief. Why art thou sad, they said; thou first of the maids of Lutha? Was he lovely as the beam of the morning, and stately in thy sight?"

CROMA.

The

CRIMOINA.

Blessed, said *Crimoina*, be the chief of *Morven*, the friend of the feeble in the day of their danger!—— But what should *Crimoina* do in her land; where every rock and hill, every tree and murmuring brook, would awake her slumbering sorrow? the youths whom I scorned, when they beheld me, would laugh, and say, where is now thy *Armor*? where is now the youth of thy love?——

We brought *Crimoina* with us to our land. We gave her fair hand to *Dargo*. But still, at times, she was sad; the secret streams, as they passed, heard on their banks her sighs.——*Crimoina*, thy day, indeed, was short. The strings of the harp are wet, while the bard repeats thy tale.

O   One

One day as we pursued the deer on Morven's darkly heath, the ships of Lochlin appeared on our seas, with all their white sails, and nodding masts. We thought it might be to demand Crimoina. "I will not fight," said Connas of the little soul, "'till I first know if that stranger loves our race. Let us pursue the boar, and dye the robe of Dargo with his blood. Then let us carry the body of her husband home, and see how she will mourn for his loss."——

We heard in an evil hour the advice of Connas: we pursued the foaming boar, and brought him low in the echoing woods. Two held him in all his foam, while Connas pierced him through with the spear.——

Dargo lay down, and we sprinkled him over with the blood: we bore him on our spears to
Crimoina;

Crimoina; and sung, as we went along, the song of
death. Connas ran before us with the skin of the
boar. I slew him, he said, with my steel; but
first his deadly tusk had pierced thy Dargo. For the
spear of the chief was broke, and the loose rock had
failed below him. .

Crimoina heard the tale of the tomb. She saw
her Dargo brought home as dead. Silent and pale
she stood, as the pillar of ice that hangs, in the season
of cold, from the brow of Mora's rock. At length
she took her harp, and touched it, soft, in praise of
her love. Dargo would rise, but we forbad 'till' the
song should cease; for it was sweet as the voice of the
wounded swan, when she sings away her soul in
death, and feels in her breast the fatal dart of the
hunter. Her companions flock, mournful, around;
they assuage her pain with their song, and bid the

O 2   ghosts

ghosts of swans convey her soul to the airy lake of the clouds. Its place is above the mountains of Morven.

"Bend," she said, "from your clouds, ye fathers of Dargo; bend and carry him to the place of your rest. And ye maids of Trenmoi's airy land, prepare the bright robe of mist for my love. O Dargo, why have I loved, why was I beloved so much! Our souls were one; our hearts grew together, and how can I survive when they are now divided? —We were two flowers that grew in the cleft of the rock; and our dewy heads, amidst sun-beams, smiled. The flowers were two; but their root was one. The virgins of Cona saw them, and turned away their foot; 'they are lonely they said,' but lovely! The deer, in his course, leaned over them; and the roe forbore to crop them. But the wild boar,

boar, relentless, came. He tore up the one with his deadly tusk. The other bends over it his drooping head; and the beauty of both, like the dry herb before the sun, is decayed. "My sun on Morven now is set, and the darkness of death dwells around me. My sun shone, how bright! in the morning; its beams it shed around me, in all its smiling beauty. But e'er evening it is set, to rise no more: and leaves me in one cold, eternal, night. Alas my Dargo! why art thou so soon set? Why is thy warm heart so soon grown cold, and thy tongue of music grown so mute!——Thy hand which so lately shook the spear in the battles front, there lies stiff and cold: and thy foot, this morning the foremost in the fatal chace, there lies dead as the earth it trod. From afar, o'er seas, and hills, and dales, have I followed 'till this day my love! thy steps.

steps.——In vain did my father look for my return; in vain did my mother mourn my absence. Their eye was often on the sea; The rocks often heard their cry. But I have been deaf, O my parents, to your voice; for my thoughts were fixed on Dargo.—— O that death would repeat on me his stroke! O that the wild boar had also torn Crimoina's breast! Then should I mourn on Morven no more, but joyfully go with my love on his cloud!——Last night I slept on the heath by thy side; is there not room this night, in thy shroud? Yes, beside thee I will lay me down; with thee, this night too, I will sleep, my love, my Dargo!"——

——We heard the faltering of her voice: we heard the faint note dying on her hand: we raised Dargo from his place. But it was too late. Crimoina was no more. The harp dropped from her hand. Her

Her soul she breathed out in the song.   She fell beside her Dargo.

He raised her tomb, with Crimora, on the shore; and hath prepared the gray stones for his own in the same place.

Since then, twice ten summers have gladdened the plains; and twice ten winters have covered with snow the woods.   In all that time, the man of grief hath lived in his cave, alone; and listens only to the song that is sad.   Often I sing to him in the calm noon, when Crimoina bends down from her flaky mist.

Dargo.

The

The RUINS of SELMA.

Awful is the silence of night. It spreads its mantle over the vale. The hunter sleeps on the heath. His gray dog stretches his neck over his knee. In his dreams he pursues the sons of the mountain, and with joy he half awakes.

Sleep on, and take thy rest, light-bounding son of the chace; Ossian will not disturb thee. Sleep on, ye sons of toil; the stars are but running their mid-way course, and Ossian alone is awake on the hills. I love to wander alone, when all is dark and quiet. The gloom of night accords with the sadness of my soul; nor can the morning sun, with all his beams, bring day to me.——

Spare thy beams then, O Sun! like the king of
Morven,

Morven, thou art too lavish of thy bounty. Dost thou not know thy light, like his, may one day fail. Spare thy lamps which thou kindlest, by thousands, in thy blue hall above; when thou thyself retirest to thy repose, below the dusky gates of the west. Why should thy lights fail, and leave thee in thy mournful halls, alone, as his friends have done to Ossian? Why mighty beam, shouldst thou waste them on Morven; when the heroes have ceased to behold them; when there is no eye to admire their green-sparkling beauty?

Morven, how have thy lights failed! like the beam of the oak in thy palaces, they have decayed, and their place is the dwelling of darkness. Thy palaces themselves, like those who rejoiced within them, are fallen on the heath, and the thick shadow of death surrounds them. Temora is fallen; Tura is an heap; and Selma is silent. The sound of their

P   shells

shells is long since past. The song of their bards, and the voice of their harps are over. A green mound of earth, a moss-clad stone lifting through it here and there its gray head, is all that preserves their memory. The mariner beholds, no more, their tall heads rising through clouds, as he bounds on the deep; nor the traveller as he comes from the desart.

——I grope for Selma. I stumble on a ruin, without any form is the heap. The heath and the rank grass grow about its stones; and the lonely thistle shakes here, in the midnight breeze, its head. I feel it heavy with the drops of night. The owl flutters around my gray hairs: she awakes the roe from his bed of moss. He bounds lightly, without fear; for he sees it is but the aged Ossian.——Roe of Selma, thy death is not in the thought of the bard. Thou hast started from the bed where often slept Fingal

and

and Oscar, and dost thou think Ossian will stain it
with his spear? No; roe of the bed of Fingal and
Oscar, thy death is not in the thought of the bard.——
I only stretch my hand to the place where hung my
fathers shield; where it hung, on high, from the roof
of Selma. But the blue-bending shell of heaven,
O Selma! is now thy only covering. I seek the
broad shield among the ruins: my spear strikes
against one of its broken bosses.——It is the boss in
which dwelt the voice of war! its sound is still
pleasant to my ear: it awakes the memory of the
days that are past; as when the breath of winds
kindles the decaying flame on the heath of hinds.
I feel the heaving of my soul. It grows like the
swelling of a flood; but the burden of age presses it
back: retire, ye thoughts of war!——Ye dark-brown
years that are past, retire. Retire with your

clanging

clanging shields, and let the soul of the aged rest.
Why should war dwell, any more, in my thoughts,
when I have forgot to lift the spear? Yes the spear
of Temora is now a staff; never more shall it strike
the sounding shield.——But it does strike against a
shield: let me feel its shake.——It is like the wasting
moon, half=consumed with the rust of years.——It
was thy blue shield, O Gaul!——The shield of the
companion of my Oscar!——But why this melting of
my soul?——Son of my love! thou hast received thy
fame.——I will retire and give the name of Gaul to
the song.——Harp of Selma, where art thou? and
where art thou Malvina? Thou shalt hear with
joy of the companion of thy Oscar.

Gaul.

Sorrows

SORROWS of CATHULH.

"Long" said Cathula, "may the sons of Fingal rejoice in their fathers fame. May they brighten in its beams in the dark ages to come, and the bard say in his song, 'He is of the race of Fingal.'——But to no son of mine shall my renown descend, a bright beam to shine around him. Conloch, son of my love! that sad night, which tore thy mother and thyself at once from my arms, rises with all its stormy horrors in my view, and wound afresh my soul. It rises before me like the sea of Inistore in that night of storms. The rocks hear the noise of its waves, and they shake, with all their woods. The spirit of the mountain roars along the fall of streams; and the dweller of Inistore fears his trembling isle may sink.

——But

But grief stops the voice of Cathula. His soul is a stream that melts, when tender thoughts are warm within.——Let me hear the sad tale, O bard, from thee. It awakes my grief; but I love it."

I hear the din of arms in Icroma. I hear, through its woods, the echo of shields. I see the blaze of swords, gleaming to the moon. I see the spear of battle lifted. The roe starts from his midnight rest, and Turlethan fears the danger.—— But why art thou afraid, roe of the mountain? Why tremblest thou, Syaro, in thy halls? Sora's king is strong, but the wind of the north is awake. Upon its cloudy wing Cathula comes, like a red angry ghost of night, when hunters tremble on Stuca. The ranks of war are broken before him, as the mail of the spider before the blast. The mighty are scattered in his presence. Sora with the clouds of night,
hath

hath fled over the sea.   He hath disappeared as the path of his ship on the deep.——Sgaro, hang up thy shield; bring down thy harp; let the daughters of Icroma rejoice.——

I hear the voice of songs in Icroma.   I hear the echo of harps in its halls.   The sword of war is sheathed.   The shield is hung on the peaceful wall, a dark orb, like the inner moon; and the spear of battle rests beside it.   The roe is glad on his rock. The virgins of Turlethan look, with joy, over their window.   The sun shines bright.   No clouds is on its beams.   But the maids observe it not; their eye is on Cathula, moving in the light of his steel: they bless that beam of brightness, from whose presence the darkness of their danger retired. "Awake, our voice," they say, "awake our harps: let our song be Carric-thura's king!"

But

But who comes forth to meet the chief? Her steps are on the dew of the morning. The tear of joy hangs forward in her eyes, like the tear of night on the bended grass, when it glitters in early sun beams. Her face of beauty is half=concealed by the wandering of her fair locks. But the morning beams look through them on the mild=blushing of her cheek, as looks the sun on the budding rose, when its colour grows in the drops of dew.——Who can this be but Rosgala? the fairest of the maids of Icroma? ——Syaro gives her to the chief who scattered the cloud of his foes.——" Cathula, were ten daughters mine, chief of heroes, I would say, be thine the choice."——

Three years on their eagle=wing, flew over the hills of Turlethan. The hawk darting on his prey moves not with a pace so silent or swift. Cathula
looks

looks back on their course, as the awakened hunter on the space he travelled over in his dream. He wonders how soon they are past. "It is time to return to Inistore, to the streamy groves of Carric=thura."——

The sails of Cathula are raised. Rosgala by turns, is glad and sorrowful. "Adieu, thou isle of my love; adieu, thou abode of my youth! My friends are on the shore: the roes look forward from their bushy rock.——But why should the tears of Rosgala flow? She goes with Carric-thura's chief." Conloch, the young pledge of their love, is in their arms.——Two streaks of light on a cloud are his fair brows. His little helm above them is of the down of fawns. Lulled by the rocking of the waves, he sleeps. In the dreams of his rest, he smiles.—— He hears the buzz of mountain bees, and thinks he

2

is

is near their store of sweet. But it is not the buzzing bee, thou dost hear, O Conloch! it is the rising wind, whistling through the ratling shrouds. But still thy smile is pleasant.——Thou lookest like the flower of Lena, when the many coloured rainbow adorns it in the day of the inconstant sun. The hunter, as, hastening to the shelter of some dark bending rock, he strides along, beholds it with a sigh; for he sees the stormy shower, riding towards it on the blast: the pillars that support it are hail.——" Flower of Lena, thou art lovely, but the tread of the storm is near thee."——

The breast of Rosgala heaves under the broken sigh, white as the foam of the waves, when the storm uplifts it, and darkness dwells around. The bright drop is in her eyes; it falls on the face of Conloch. With the pressing of her lip, she wipes it away.

away. He awakes and sees the storm. He wonders what it means; and shrinking, clings to the bosom of Rosgala. She, over him, spreads her skirt, as spreads the eagle of Lora her dark wings, wide, over her young, when they shrink in their head from the hail, and hear the voice of storms.——"Fear not, child of my love," said Rosgala; "for thy father is nigh us."——Nor be thou thyself afraid, said Cuthula; I know the sea of Inistore. Often have I rode its deep, when louder was the roar of its waves. Rosgala asks for Inistore; but it is distant. The sea hides it behind its hills of foam. Mixed with the noise of waves, rise, at times, the sighs of the fair.——

Now descends on the deep, dark=skirted night. The thunder is in her course. The streamy lightning bursts, dark=red from her womb. Spirits feel its

flames.

flames. Their shrieks are heard in the mid-air.
They rush to quench their half-burnt robes in the deep.
The billows roar, with all their whales.——The
moon hears the noise within her house of clouds, and
she is afraid to lift her head above the hill. The
stars wrap their heads in the mantle of Lano's mist.
At times, they look, trembling, through the window
of their clouds; but, quick, draw back their wandering
hair.——They are like the hunter on the heath, who
shoots out, at times, his head, but will not venture
forth from his booth till the storm is over.——Hunter
of the roe of the mountain, thou art on the heath on
shore; O that Rosgala was there!

But what voice did you hear that night, ye
rocks of Toroma; when on the deep was she, to
whose harp you often echoed? Did you listen to the
roar of waves at your feet, or to the thunder that
rolled

rolled in the blasted head of your pines? Louder than either of these, rose in your ear the cries of Sulingorma. She is wildly sad, for her daughter is on the deep with her child. She stands on the dark rock, careless of the beating storm. White billows breaking on the distant deep, deceive her oft for sails.——Mother of Rosgala, retire from the storm of night; thy daughter does not hear thy cries.

Retiring, she soon turns back to view once more the main. A wandering bark, descending into the creek, is half=perceived. "Oh! art thou safe my child!"——

"What voice is that on the rock?" says the mariner; "my mates take down your sails."

The voice of joy mixed with fear again is up, "Rosgala! art thou safe?"

"It is the cry," says the mariner, "of the fair ghost

ghost that we saw upon the deep: behold it there!——
Come, O ghost, on moon-beams to our dreams, when
the night is calm, and the storm is over!"

Sulingorma hears his voice, and sad, retires.
The rocks reply to the name of Rosgala.

But Rosgala is on the sea of Inistore. The
stragling ray of a distant oak travels there over the
deep. Cuthula beheld his love, like a fair virgin
ghost in its beam. In her arms he beheld his son.
He looked like a star in the bosom of the bended
moon, when her face is almost hid in grief, and the
darkness of her countenance growing. He beheld
them: but he was sad, and his half=stifled sigh
arose. The passing breeze bore it to the ear of Rosgala.
Why that sigh, she said, my love? the night on
the deep is dark, but the storm will soon be over. The
moon will come forth in her silent beauty; her steps

on

on the mountain will be lovely. The stars will shew
their blue=sparkling eyes in the clouds, and the
winds will retire from the sea of Inistore. Nor is
Inistore far distant: is not that the light of its
halls?" ——

Light of the soul of Cathula, the storm will soon
be past; and the light of Inistore, amidst blue,
calm waves, arise. But what is night, or storm,
or distance of Inistore, to Cathula, while he beholds
the face of beauty, with all thy calm of soul? ——
Let me behold the face of my love, O beam! and
I will bless thee, tho' thou dost come from Sora's
hall; though thou hast brought me so nigh his
shelving rocks." ——

Too nigh them art thou brought indeed, O
Cathula; on their edge thy skiff, in two, is divided.
The chief climbs the oozy rock. Rosgala and his

son

son are in his arms. But no shelter, save from cold sea-weeds, is there. It is at times the habitation of seals.

"The land, my love, is nigh. My strength, I know, can reach it. On its shore I may find some boat that shall convey us from Sora's wrath, before the light shall arise. Rest thou here, Rosgala. The storm is lower. The stars look over the edge of their broken clouds, and the moon lifts her pale head, through the distant tree. They will soon shew thee the path of my return. Rest here my love Rosgala! —Ye lights of heaven, shine on my love; ye spirits on their beams, dwell with her on her rock. When you hear her say, 'Cathula, what delays thy return?' tell her you behold the steps of my coming.

"Come thou mayest," said Rosgala; "but ah! I fear the billows roar. Some blast may raise it high;

high; or some angry ghost may, again, embroil it in its course. But thou shalt come, my love:—— and yet I fear.—The sea may grow; the shades may depart; or Sora awake e'er thou dost come.—— But no; my love shall soon return. Spirits of my fathers! guard Cathula."—He went; he searched the shore: but no boat is nigh. He runs in search of it far. The thought of his soul is on the oozy rock with Rosgala.

What shall that helpless mourner do? Her eye is towards the darkly shore; but no Cathula comes. The waves grow upon her rock. They gather about her feet. But, Conloch, thou art not wet; thou art lifted high in her arms.

"What detains thee, my love?—Have the waves stopped thy course to the shore; or have the boats of Sora been distant far?—O that thou wert

R   ashore

ashore, my child! 'Tis for thee that trembles thus the soul of Rosgala."

She ties him on Cathula's shield. A withered tree comes, wandering on the waves, to her rock.—— On its top she fixes Conloch.

Shall I awake thee, Conloch? No, thy cries would pierce my soul, like darts. Safe thou mayest reach the shore; and Sora's king may have pity. Or, thy father perhaps may find thee. But ah! my child, thy father I fear is not. On that cloud his spirit waits for mine.——Stay, Cathula; thy love is coming.

A higher surge comes, white=tumbling, over the rock. In its cold bosom it folds Rosgala. "Farewel, O my Conloch!"

Too late, Cathula comes in the boat of Sora. He looks for the rock: but no rock, dark=rising

above

above the wave, is seen.——" The growing sea hath covered its oozy top! No Rosgala; no Conloch is here! O that the same wave had inclosed Cathula! Then, Rosgala, would we smile in death; Conloch would we clasp in our arms; his tender frame should not be hurt by rocks.——Shall Cathula live or die?"

The light, half=mixt with darkness, breaks on Sora's hills. A small isle is near. A watery cave is under its rock; and over its mouth there bends, in its own gray coat of moss, an aged oak. It is here Cathula waits for night. It comes with all its stars. Rosgala descends on the soul of her love. She comes soft=gliding on the face of the deep.—— Her robe is of the white mist that rises on Cona, when morning=dews are melting in the beams of the sun. But her tresses still are wet: they drop like

the

the dew of roses on the bank of their slow-rolling river. —She tells him of her fate; she tells him how she laid Conloch on his shield. ‘ But let Cathula,’ she says, ‘ awake, and fly safe to Inistore.’

He rose. In silent grief over the waves he came. But since, he is often sad. His tears in the morning flow for Rosgala; and his sighs in the evening are heard for Conloch.

Catbul.

Heroism

HEROISM of MORNA.

Carril came with his harp.   Its sound was soft as the gliding of ghosts on the banks of Lora; when they hide themselves in the white mist of noon, and their sound is on the gale of the stream.——Move in silence, stream of night, that we may listen to the song of the bard.

"Over Lora of streams there bends an oak.—— Below it, one lone thistle lifts, between two stones, its head.   It sheds, in the passing stream, its drops of dew.   Two ghosts are seen there at noon, when the sun is on the plain, and silence reigns in Morven. One is thy ghost, aged Urad; thy hair wanders, a whiter mist, over two clouds that form thy darkned eyes.——And who is that in the cloud of snow before
thee

thee? Who but that fair huntress of the roe thy daughter?——

" The youths of Lora were at the chace: they were spreading the feast in the booth of the desart, Colgor saw them, and came to Lora in secret, like the torrent that rushes, sudden, from the hill, when no shower is seen by the sunny vale.——'Daughter of Ural, thou must go with Colgor. The thongs must confine thy father. He might strike the shield. The youths might hear its sound in the desart?——

" Colgor, I love thee not. Leave me here with my father. None is with him. His eyes are dark, and his gray hairs are lonely.

" Colgor would not hear. The daughter of Ural must go with him; but her steps on the heath are mournful. She moves, sad, like the mist of
showers,

showers, when the sun is dim, and the valley of streams is silent. A roe bounds on the heath; he steals below them towards a small stream. His brown sides, at times, appear through the green, rank ferns.——Colgor, give me that bow; I have learned to pierce the deer.——He gave the bow. She drew the string. Colgor fell.——She returned to Lora, and the soul of her father was glad. The evening of his life was like the departure of the sun on the mountain of spring; like the leaf of autumn, when it drops in the silent vale. The days of Morala, on the hills were many; in death she rested, in peace, with her father.——Over Lora of streams there bends an oak. Below it are two beds. One, Ural; is thine; and thine, daughter of the bow, is the other beside it.——

Duthona.

The CHIEF of FEYGLEN.

As the rolling of the huge stone down the haughty brow of Morcraig, when the affrightened flocks stretch every nerve to shun the coming danger, and the torn heath is round the whirling of its rapid journey; so bold, so strong, so terrible was the son of Feyglen, in the fields of death. The mighty saw the coming of his strength, and they sank beneath the weight of his sword. The feeble fled the danger they could not meet. Albin's sons rejoiced in his deeds as they filled his footsteps behind.

Such was the rolling of his might, when the shield of Swanvil met the point of his spear. Stop——said the chief of Lochlin; and let the collected strength of thy arm be in the darting of thy lance.

Strong

Strong is the shield before thee, and mighty is the arm that supports the glittering wing of steel. My sword triumphs not in the fall of little men. I mourn when feeble foes are before me. But thy fame is great, O warrior! Thy coming in battle is like the coming of a hundred streams, when their foaming journey is down the shaggy brow of the haughty rock. We have both been renowned; but a gray stone will lift its mossy head on the hill before the storms of other years. The hunter, as he passeth, will cry, ' Here the mighty fought.' If my sword becomes thine, send it, O warrior, to Savina. Her soft=rolling eye meets the rising sun on the plains of Tauron. The maid will pierce her bosom with the point, and our ghosts will rejoice in the land of clouds.

No steel from me shall pierce the breast of the lovely

S

lovely, said Donran.   Yield, warrior, and return in safety to Savina.   Her mild eye will view thee with joy, and bless the hand that spared thee in battle.

In vain hast thou spoke, son of pride! Persuasive sweetness is not thine.——Thy words are feeble, like the blast that holds a contest with a stubborn rock. Did the points of five hundred spears meet my shield; did the strength of a hundred warriors raise each spear; did the meteors of death fly around me, as the fire of heaven, when bursting clouds roll in horror through the angry sky;——yet would I not yield.

Two blue steels rose in wrath.   Donran stood alone.   Many sons of Lochlin came behind.   A bloody stream was seen. Swanvil stopped the unequal strife.——The thoughts of the valiant darted on his soul.   He cursed the coward's spear.

Donran

Dowran fell not alone. On either side they bleed. The spear is the pillar of his bloody side. His shield rolls on earth. Terrible are the threatening looks of the hero. The foe viewed, and trembled. Ghosts fled from the fallen around. Terrified, they mount the clouds that pass. We heard the warriors sighs. Too late we raised the spear. Many sank with the hero: the rest fled in haste. Swanvil scorned our strength. He sought the sword of Scarlaw.—— But what son of song can relate the meeting of the two chiefs! Rocks spoke the words of steel. The broken shield sank from Swanvil. His spear shall rise no more.——The race of Lochlin fled. The blast is their shield, as they mount blue rolling waves.

The aged Feyglen listened in the anguish of his soul to the tale of woe. A tear wanders down his

S 2   withered

wrinkled cheek. He clasps his hands in grief. Many groans come forth.——Mournful are his words. A blast has withered the plains. A cloud has darkened the sky.—— Joy meet the soul of the valiant. Never shall the spear of my fathers rise in battle! I shall vanish, like a dim shadow that wanders before the rays of the moon. No son of mine shall raise the huge stone near my narrow dwelling.—— My name shall cease to sound in the years that approach. My departure shall be as the blast that flies unheeded over the mountains.——A sudden beam of comfort rushes on my soul. Sulalin, image of her who was lovely! reach me thy white hand.—— Gather thy waving locks from the wind, Dry thy father's cheek with thy soft ringlets. A tear from thy blue eyes shall bathe my memory on the mountains. A plant may rise from thy side. The spear of

Feyglen

Feyglen may yet rise in battle.——A ray of comfort rushes on the wretched. Forgot I shall not be, soft beam of youth!

The chief stretched forth his hand. But he stretched it to the wind.——No white arm received it: No soft voice was heard.——A blast that withers rushed through his nerves. He trembled as a feeble twig before the haughty storm. Breeze after breeze saluted the woods; but the gray-haired Feyglen listened in vain.——The soft voice of Sulalin is not mingled with the wind.

A black cloud is gathering in the east. Why do the oaks bend their green heads before it? Why do the rocks rear their cliffy brows to meet it in wrath?——A hundred sighs are heard, as it flies in surly speed over the mountains. The tears of heroes pour forth before it. The death of the lovely has
darkened

darkened its gloomy aspect. The fold of the cloud is the wing of a tale of woe.

Bathe thy dim eyes in tears, chief of the aged locks!——She who was bright in thy hall, sleeps cold in death. The ghost of the virgin rose on the fairest beam of the morning. The son of Scarlaw is the partner of her flight to the land of clouds. Piercing are thy words, son of the mournful tale.——But the eyes of Shearvan have already shed all their tears: his feeble breast hath already poured forth all its sighs. The rocks of Ardven have heard it, and returned their groans of pity.——But thou travellest in thy mirth, O son of heaven! regardless of my woes. And long mayest thou rejoice in thy blue=fields, thou brightest tenant of the sky! The children of an hundred glens look with the eye of expectation for the coming forth of thy beauty, though the

darkened

darkened eyes of Shearvan refuse to admit thy beams.
But some day, like me, they will look in vain.
Stormy clouds will wrap thee in their dark folds,
when the battles of many ghosts are in thy land.——
Thou wilt then, like me, weep; but the wrathful
winds will not regard thee.

But roll on, in all the strength of thy brightness,
fair-haired traveller of the sky! Carry with thee
all thy smiles to cheer the valiant who sleep in the
isle of peace. The course of thy speed all day is
towards them. The angry storms terrify not thee.
Sullen clouds may veil thy beauty; but they cannot
oppose thee. The couch of thy repose is with the
ghosts of our fathers. There thou layest down thy
fair head to rest; and the feeble children of the
wind sleep among the golden locks of thy beauty.

O Sulalin! when other ghosts are asleep, steal
thou

thou in secret to the dreams of thy father. Tell me
if Culoina has forget me in the season of my grey
hairs; she who had seen me in the days of my strength.
But my strength is fled, like a blast to the desart:
my friends have vanished as the mist on Ardven.
Heavy are mine eyes of age! leave me to my rest, ye
tenants of the hill.——Come, Sulalin! to the dreams
of my slumbers.

Such was the words of the chief in the season of
his woe. The voice of his grief was heard no more:
his sighs ceased to mingle with the wind. His tomb
lifts its head high on Ardven. The traveller listens
to his tale with streaming eyes:——For he fell like the
last tree of the forest, when no plant remains to tell the
place where it stood.

Chief of Feyglen.

The

The DEATH of OSCAR.

Why openest thou afresh the spring of my grief, O son of Alpin, inquiring how Oscar fell? My eyes are blind with tears; bu. memory beams on my heart. How can I relate the mournful death of the head of the people! Chief of the warriors, Oscar, my son, shall I see thee no more.

He fell as the moon in a storm; as the sun from the midst of his course, when clouds rise from the waste of the waves, when the blackness of the storm innraps the rocks of Arannider. I like an ancient oak on Morven, I moulder alone in my place. The blast hath lopped my branches away; and I tremble at the wings of the north. Chief of

I   the

the warriors, Oscar, my son! Shall I see thee
no more?

But, son of Alpin, the hero fell not harmless
as the grass of the field; the blood of the mighty was
on his sword, and he travelled with death through
the ranks of their pride. But Oscar, thou son
of Caruth; thou hast fallen low! No enemy fell
by thy hand. Thy spear was stained with the blood
of thy friend.

Dermid and Oscar was one: they reaped the
battle together. Their friendship was strong as
their steel; and death walked between them to the
field. They came on the foe like two rocks falling
from the brows of Ardven. Their swords were
stained with the blood of the valiant: warriors
fainted at their names. Who was equal to Oscar
but Dermid? and who to Dermid, but Oscar?

They

They killed mighty Dargo in the field; Dargo who never fled in war. His daughter was fair as the morn; mild as the beam of night. Her eyes like two stars in a shower: her breath, the gale .of spring: her breasts, as the new-fallen snow floating on the moving heath. The warriors saw her, and loved; their souls were fixed on the maid. Each loved her as his fame; each must possess her, or die. But her soul was fixed on Oscar; the son of Caruth was the youth of her love. She forgot the blood of her father; and loved the hand that slew him.

Son of Caruth, said Dermid, I love; O Oscar, I love this maid. But her soul cleaveth unto thee; and nothing can heal Dermid. Here, pierce this bosom Oscar; relieve me, my friend, with thy sword.——

My

My sword, son of Diaran, shall never be stained with the blood of Dermid.

Who then is worthy to slay me, O Oscar son of Caruth? Let not my life pass away unknown. Let none but Oscar slay me. Send me with honour to the grave, and let my death be renowned.

Dermid, make use of thy sword; son of Diaran, wield thy steel Would that I fell with thee! that my death came from the hand of Dermid!

They fought by the brook of the mountain, by the streams of Branno. Blood singed the running water, and curdled round the mossy stones. The stately Dermid fell; he fell, and smiled in death.

And fallest thou, son of Diaran, fallest thou by Oscar's hand! Dermid who never yielded in war, thus do I see thee fall.——He went, and
returned

returned to the maid of love; he returned, but she perceived his grief.

Why that gloom, son of Caruth? what shades thy mighty soul?

Though once renowned for the bow, O maid, I have lost my fame—Fixed on a tree by the brook of the hill, is the shield of the valiant Gormur, whom I slew in battle. I have wasted the day in vain, nor could my arrow pierce it.

Let me try, son of Caruth, the skill of Dargo's daughter. My hands were taught to the bow; my father delighted in my skill.

She went. He stood behind the shield. Her arrow flew, and pierced his breast.

Blessed be that hand of snow; and blessed that bow of yew! Who but the daughter of Dargo, was worthy to slay the son of Caruth? Lay me in the earth

earth, my fair one; lay me by the side of Dermid.

Oscar! the maid replied, I have the soul of the mighty Dargo. Well pleased I can meet death. My sorrow I can end.——She pierced her white bosom with the steel. She fell; she trembled; and died.——

By the brook of the hill their graves are laid; a birch's unequal shade covers their tomb. Often on their green earthen tombs the branchy sons of the mountain feed, when mid=day is all in flames, and silence over all the hills.

Temora.

The

The CAVE of CREMTA.

Cold was the blast from the regions of frost, and fatal proved the surly offspring of the north, to the feeble reapers of the flowery field. Legions of insects perished by the poisonous breath of the reigning storm. The feathered songster stopped the warbling note at the frowning approach of the rude intruder.

The father of light withdrew his circular presence beyond the southern hill. Feeble were his oblique rays, which, half intercepted, dimly shone o'er the tops of the mountains. The congealer of the liquid stream, who annually retires beyond the northern ocean, further than the cleavers of the waves can trace his rapid flight, returned from his summer expedition. He now began to usurp his tyrannical

reign

reign, in the absence of the sire of brightness, whose presence he would have shunned with a speed equal to his who flies from impending destruction. Nature trembles at the approach of the cruel spoiler; and the feeble among her sons fall victims to the resistless oppressor. He locks up the stream from the shaggy tenants of the forest; and the finny inhabitants of the flood dwell in darkness, while in vain they search for the intercepted day.

Such was the season, and dismal was the visage of the mountains, when Liachan led his six sons to the cave of Creyla. The frozen offspring of the sky had closed up the unfrequented entrance: but an impending cliff, which projected from the mother rock, contended with the passing blast; and the murmuring noise pointed out the door of the cave to the trembling leader of the youthful band.

Thrice

Thrice did Liachan bless the lonely cavern as he entered, and thrice did the flinty pillars of the rock, with their echoing voices, return the friendly salutation through the hollow centre. The well=known cave recalled to the remembrance of the sage the companions of his youth, when he retired from danger to this gloomy cell. A deep sigh issued from his aged bosom, when his mind rolled back on the deeds of other years. He dropt the tear of affection to the memory of his departed friends.

Draw hither, my sons, and listen with the ears of attention to the unfeigned words of Liachan. Learn from them to avoid the follies of youth; so shall the tears of age never bedew your wrinkled cheeks.——

The arm of my father Tomduth was the shield of my feeble years. In safety I rose behind it, like

U

the

the tender shrub that rears its soft head near the stately oak. The blast on either side frowns in vain: the strength of many years meets it. The course of its flight is backwards, and the sound of its wrath is heard on distant rocks. So fled the foes of Inver from the sword of Tomduth.

As Trombia in her hollow bed gathers her liquid strength from the fertile newes of a thousand crystal rills, extending their winding arms round the heathy mountains; so gathered the evening, the flocks of Tomduth to the plains of Elian.

The meeting of warriors was in the hall of Inver. Benvel struck the harp to the fame of departed heroes, and implanted the image of valour in the rising generation. Hospitality stood at the outer gate, and with the finger of invitation waved to the traveller as he passed on his way. The chief stood
unequalled

unequalled in wisdom and valour. The venerable raised his voice to proclaim it. But where is the strength of the chief? Where the music of the bard? ——Tomduth lies unactive in the tomb of Kilmore. Eternal muteness reigns on the quivering tongue of Benvel. The father of the song shall no more be heard at the feast of Balden.

The chief retired not like a misty cloud before the face of the blast. He foresaw his fall; and his son received the words of instruction.

Liachan, I am old.——The meteors of death have warned me to depart. I go to visit the ghosts of our fathers. Come to the rocks of Creyla: receive an asylum sacred to the chief of Inver.

The warrior was bright in the armour of his fathers: but the liquid sons of sorrow rushed to my eyes, and concealed him from my eager view. My

throat

throat denied a passage to the thoughts of my breast; they were big, and could only find their passage by halves. Words, at last were formed from the broken accents.——We passed through the glens of Elian.——The wind of the north came rushing o'er the heath, and rattled on the armour of Tomduth as it passed: the armour of Tomduth regarded it not; and we reached the Cave of Creyla, as if quietness had been the ruler of the night.

Tomduth was tall: he leaned upon his half-erected spear as he entered. The spear saluted the threshold. Fire fled the daughter of the rock, at the embrace of the steel. The flinty sisters of the cave echoed a chorus to the sound, to welcome the chief, the only visitor of the lonely cell.

This cave, said Tomduth, is hitherto unknown to the sons of the heath. Let it protect the feeble of
thy

thy race, if thy foes shall urge the contest; but seek
not thy own safety in concealment. Fly not in the face
of danger; nor tremble when the meteors of death are
around thee. Be not the first to draw, nor the
first to sheath the sword. Avoid not the combat with
the mighty; but shun the ignoble contest. Let thy
face be to the strong, and thy back to the feeble foe.

Make not the daughter of Dungeal the mother of
thy sons. Poison not the offspring of thy loins by
mingling in their composition the juice of a baneful
plant. Let the milky food of their infant days be
derived from a pure fountain: so shall they be
defended from the weeds which corrupt the heart.

The words of instruction were ended; and the
daughters of the rock ceased to enforce the precepts of
the chief: muteness was in the cave; and nought was
heard

heard but the voice of night, which in hoarse accents saluted the rocks as it passed.

The tomb of the chief rose on Kilmore; Benvel's song of woe was heard round the ourd. The tear of beauty bedewed the cheek of the virgin: warriors shook their dejected heads as they met. Rocks joined in pity the sound of grief: each breeze was the messenger of a tale of woe.

Stormal was the stately son of Dungeal. He led the warriors of his father to battle. The arrow of random fled not from his bow. She continued her journey to the distant mark; and fatal proved her arrival to the breast of the foe.

Sulgorma was the seat of a thousand beauties. Many heroes wooed the maid; but the thoughts of her dreams were of Liachan, though I regarded not the kindly glances of her blue eyes. So look the

wishing

nishing eyes of the bewildered traveller in search of the intercepted beams, when the loaded sky leans her burden of mist on the hills of Minaig.   But the ungrateful tenant of the enlighted vale, views, with eyes of indifference, the bountiful favours of the Father of Light.——

The feast of Balden was spread at Dunzeal. Bards sung the tales of love.——I forgot the words of Instruction, and opened my eyes to the beauties of Sulgorma.   I looked in kindness on the maid, and saw her clothed in loveliness.   Our meetings were often in secret, and we thought of each other in the season of dreams.

Benvel saw my love for Sulgorma, and the friendly resentment of his breast awaked.———Son of Tomduth, said the bard, departed is the fame of thy house! The words of instruction thou hast

regarded

regarded as the blast that flies over the mountains.
—Luachos, of the race of bards, bring my harp,
and place my partner of danger by my side. I
will wander to other lands. Too long hath my song
been heard at Inver.

Son of the days of old, said I, weighty are thy
words. Feeble is the breath of unripened years; and
fruitless are her efforts when arrogantly she endeavours
to oppose the offspring of thy mouth. Thy tongue
has given birth to piercing words; but Liachan stands
reprieved by the frowns of friendship. Were the
beauties of Sulgorma as the sun of heaven in the
infancy of day, never should she shine in the hall
of Inver.

Malalin of the graceful eye, the beautiful
daughter of the chief of Erwin, mourned the fall
of her father. The emblem of grief sat on her cheek.
I blessed

I blessed the maid of woe, and brought her to the hall of my fathers.——Stormal heard the secret sigh of Sulgorma, and raised his threatening spear. Many were his warriors, and weighty was his sword in the day of death. I gathered the strength of Inver to oppose him; but feeble proved my arm in every contest; for my spear was raised against an injured foe.——Many were the years of our strife, and many the death of our warriors. When the force of Inver failed, I brought Mealalin to the cave of Creyla. The safety of my sons was her care. I slew the deer of the desart, and carried them to our feast.——But blessed be the soul of her who feasts no more in my cave!—When the daughter of Ervin retired to the land of ghosts, I carried my sons to the tower of the woody vale, and Gildea wiped the tear of grief from mine eye; by the side of the friendly stream.

Cave of Creyla.

X

Ronnan

RONNAN and SULMINA.

Ronnan hears the song of battle, and the joy of his countenance returns. He strikes his shield. His heroes are round him, a thick cloud, the gathering of the tempest on Dura.

As the spirit of night moves, with the collected blast of heaven in his course, when he prepares to pour his force on the groves of Ardven; when oaks hear its sound at a distance, and, trembling for its approach, already shake their leaves :—— So rushed Ronnan to the battle at the head of Heroes.——Nor less terrible is the course of Lava. The sound of his people is like thunder in clouds, when Lara's fields are dismal. A thousand helmets, nod on high. like a grove in flames is the blaze of spears.

But

But who shall tell the rage of battle?——Thou hast seen two black rocks rolling from opposite hills to meet in the vallies below; a cloud of smoke rises behind, and follows the tract of each: such was the terrible onset of the people. Swords clash, and shields resound: heads and helmets fall: the dead are mixed with the dying: blood runs in a thousand streams; and the spirits of fallen heroes ascend on their airy smoke. See! to the edge of every cloud they cling, as clings the bur to the eagle's wing, when she leaves the valley of dun=roes, and flies to Moma's cloudy top.

But what eagles are these two, that still contend with rustling wings on the heath? No gray bird, no red crested cock, is the prey for which they strive, as from side to side they bound, and pour death in streams from their steel.——See! one stoops on his

X 2

knee

knee. His shield supports the half-fallen chief, as the rock supports the pine, which the storm has half-overturned on Dunora. Yield thy spear, said Ronnan; restore my beloved Sulmina. I seek not the death of my foes, when they lie before me on earth.

Yield I must, Lava replied, for my blood is shed; the stream of my life hath failed.——Sulmina must be thine. Behind that rock in her cave she rests.—— She looks down from its door on a blue stream, where waves an aspen tree.——Sulmina must be thine, but let her raise my tomb, for she was the love of Lava the unhappy. He ceased. He sunk on his shield; and his people fled. Ronnan bid us spare them in their flight, as swift, he ascended the rock to find the place of his love.——The blue stream he finds; and the cave on its woody bank. But no Sulmina is there. The lone wind sounds in the empty womb of the

the rock. The withered leaf wanders there, on its rustling wing; and no tract is found, but that of the lonely fox. "Where art thou, O Sulmina, my love! dost thou hide thyself from Ronnan?—— Come, Sulmina, from thy secret place; come, my love: it is thy Ronnan calls thee!"

But thou callest in vain son of grief; no one replies to thy voice, save the rock and the ecchoing stream. At length, the howling of his dog is heard in the field of fallen heroes. Thither he turns. There he finds Sulmina. She had rushed to the battle to aid her Ronnan. But death on the point of a wandering arrow, came; its barbed head is in her breast of snow. The sparkling light of her eyes is become dim; the rose of her cheek is faded.———Ronnan pale as her own half-breathless corse, falls on her neck, as drops the ivy when its oak

hath

hath failed. Sulmina half-opens her heavy eyes.
The peaceful shade of death closes them again, well
pleased to see her Ronnan.——Long we bended
our heads in silent grief, and shed our tears around
Sulmina. At length the slow steps of Runma
came. He spoke the words of the aged.——"Will
sorrow recall the dead; will the cries of the living
dispel their heavy slumbers? No; they still sleep on,
careless of the cry of the mourner.——But they are
only gone a little before us to the land of their rest.
A few more fleeting days, on their swift-gliding
stream shall pass, and our steps shall be in air with
our friends. Do you not already see the cloud-
skirted robe prepared for Runma. Nor shall
Ronnan be long behind. The stream of grief washes
the bank on which his beauty grows. The young tree
that lifts there its green head, already half-bends over it

in

in its fall.   Let, then, our deeds of fame be many, while we can; and let not our winged days be wasted in mourning.——Grief is a calm dream, O Ronnan! the steps of its course are silent.   But it undermines in secret the beauteous flower that grows on its green bank, drooping it hangs its withered head; it falls while its leaf is but tender.——— Ronnan arose; but still he was sad.   He gave the halls of Lava to Runma and the son of Lamor; Fermor and the scout of night he left to defend them.——We brought Sulmina over the wave in Ronnan's ship; and here we raised amidst sighs her gray stone.   Here too rests the youthful Ronnan whose arm was once so strong; whose form was once so fair.   His days were sad and few, on the hill; he did not long survive his beloved.   Under that moss=clad stone he was laid, where grows the

rustling

rustling grafs. He rests beside his Sulmina. One
lone thistle bends between their two gray stones, its
head, and sheds on either side its aged beard.——
Often when I sit here to the glimmering light of the
moon, I see the faint forms of the two on its
watry beams. I take my harp, and sing their
praise, glad they depart on the wings of wind.

Thou sittest by thine own blue stream, son of Azar,
Why so silent, dost thou not know the sons of fame
are around thee.

Cathlava.

Civa=dona.

𝕮𝕴𝕯𝕬=𝕯𝕺𝕹𝕬:

Dost thou not remember, Malvina, the beauty of the stranger, when the brightness of the day arose, and the sun shone on the heathy hill? Yes, for thou didst attend her, on thy steed to Ardven, and then pursued the chace with the king. It was then we beheld the beauty of Civa=dona, when thou didst retire, like the moon, behind thy mountains. She shone, like a bright star over the broken edge of a cloud; but who could admire that star, when the full, un=clouded moon was seen?——Yet the star of Gormluba was fair.——White were the rows within her lips: and like the down of the mountain, under her new robe, was her skin. Circle on circle formed her fairest neck. Like hills beneath their soft=snowy

Y   fleeces

fleeces, rose her two breasts of love. The melody of music was in her voice. The rose beside her lip was not red: nor white beside her hand, the foam of streams.——Maid of Gormluba, who can describe thy beauty! Thy eye brows mild and narrow, were of a darkish hue; thy cheeks were like the red berry of the mountain ash. Around them were scattered the blossoming flowers on the bough of the spring.—— The yellow hair of Civa=dona, was like the gilded top of a mountain, when golden clouds look down upon its green head, after the sun has retired.——Her eyes were bright as sun=beams, and altogether perfect was the form of the fair.——Heroes beheld and blessed her.

Chief of Scarlaw.

COLGUL and CHLMORA.

Son of the morning, the steps of thy rising are lovely; the lifting of thy yellow hair above the eastern mountain. The hills smile when they behold thee; and the glittering vales, with all their blue streams, are glad. The trees lift their green=growing heads through the shower to meet thee; and all the bards of the grove salute, with their morning=song, thy coming.——But whither does the night fly, on its dark-eagle wing, when it sees thy face; and where is the place of darkness? whither do the stars retire from thy presence, and where is the cave in which they hide their trembling beauty? Into what desart dost thou chace them, when thou climbest the mountains of heaven; and pursuest them, like a

Y 2

mighty

mighty hunter, through the blue fields of the sky?——
Son of heaven, the steps of thy course are lovely,
when thou travellest above, in thy brightness, and
scatterest from thy face the storms. The departure
of thy yellow hair is lovely, when thou sinkest in the
western wave; and lovely is the hope of thy coming.
In the mists of night thou never losest thy course;
and tempests in the troubled deep, in vain oppose thee.
At the call of the morning thou art always ready,
and the light of thy return is pleasant; it is pleasant,
but I see it not; for thou dost not dispel the night
from the eye of the bard.

As the rolling of rocks from the top of hills; as the
noise of waves when the tempest is high; or as groves
when their dry hair is seized by flames through night.
Such was the terror of the path of Trathal.——Colgul
and he were two mountain streams in the strife: the
sound

sound of their steel was like the echo in the narrow vale, when its green pines are felled.——Dreadful is their battle! Trathal is a storm that overcomes the grove, and a wave that climbs the shore is Colgul.—— But the eyes of Colgul reel in mist, as lights on his helmet the massy spear. Corran stands without his shield, like a rock which the lightning has bored. Duchonnis stops with his hand the red stream of his breast, and leans his back to a broken tree. The helmet of Crusollis glitters between his feet, with one half his head, before he falls: and the gray hair of Tual=arma is trampled in blood and dust, by the crowding feet of heroes.

Colgul scatters with his red eyes the cloud.—— He sees his people in their blood around. Like the dark shadow of Lego's mist, he comes in silence behind the king, but he comes not unperceived. Trathal

turns

turns, Colgul flies. His steps are to the boat, and Trathal in his strength pursues him. A thousand arrows aim at the king. By one of them Colgul is pierced. He falls upon the shore when one hand hath hold of the boat. Trathal leaps into its dark womb, and turns upon the people of Colgul. He turns; but a blast drives him into the deep, and he bounds in the midst of his fame with joy.

The spouse of Trathal had remained in her house, two children rose, with their fair locks, about her knees. They bend their ears above the harp, as she touched, with her white hand, its trembling strings. She stops. They take the harp themselves; but cannot find the sound which they admired——Why they said does it not answer us? shew us the string wherein dwells the song. She bids them search for

it

it till she returns. Their little fingers wander among the wires.

Sulin-dona looks for her love. The hour of his return is past. "Trathal, where dost thou wander among streams; where has thy path erred among woods? from this height may I behold thy tall form; may I see the smiling joy of thy ruddy face. Between thy yellow locks of youth, thou lookest like the morning sun."

She ascended the hill, like a white cloud of the melted dew, when it rises on early beams from the secret vale, and rushes scarce wave their brown-lifted heads. She saw a skiff bounding on the deep: she saw on the shore a grove of spears.——"Surely they must be foes who lift them; and Trathal is alone. Can one tho' strong contend with thousands? Her cries ascend the rock. The vales reply with

all

all their streams. Youths rush from their mountains, and wildly tremble in their steps for their king.——— They thought of rushing on the people of Colgul in their wrath; but Trathal raised on the deep his voice, and bade them stop the spear. They rejoiced when they heard the king, and saw him turn to the shore his ship. They gathered about Colgul; but his face was dark, and the flame of his eye had failed.——— His people stood motionless around; but many of them had strewed the brown heath, like dry leaves on autumn's dusky plain, when tempests shake the oak. We help them to raise their tombs; and first we dig the grave of Colgul.——A youth stoops to place beside the spear. The mail in rising, drops from two heaps of snow. Calmora falls beside her love.——Sulin-dona as she came, beheld her pale. She knew the

daughter

daughter of Cornglas. Her tears fall over her in the grave. She praised the fair of Sorna.

"Daughter of beauty, thou art low. A strange shore receives thy corse. But thou wilt rejoice on thy cloud, for thou sleepest in the tomb with Colgul. The ghosts of Morven will open their halls to the young stranger, when they see thee approach. Heroes around the feast of dim shells, in the midst of clouds, shall admire thee; and virgins in thy praise shall touch the harp of mist. Thou wilt rejoice, O Calmora; but thy father in Sorna will be sad. His steps of age will wander on the shore. The roar of the wave will come from the distant rock.——' Calmora,' lifting his gray head, he will say, ' is that thy voice?——The son of the rock alone will reply. Retire to thy house, O Cornglass, retire from the stormy shore; her steps

Z   with

with Colgul are high on clouds. On moon=beams, she may come perhaps, to thy dreams, when silence reigns in Sorna. Daughter of beauty, thou art low but thou sleepest in the tomb with Colgul.

Such was the song over Calmora; but who could speak in praise of Colgul? Often have their ghosts sighed on the mournful mists that creep along the tombs. But thou seest them not, O sun: they come only when darkness covers the hills: But thou seest the ghost of Trathal:——Often does he stalk in thy beams at noon, when the hills are covered with mist. Thou delightest to shed thy beams on the clouds which enrobes the brave, and to spread thy rays round the tombs of the valiant. Often do I feel them on the bed of Trenmor, and even now thou warmest the gray stone of Trathal. Thou rememberest the heroes, O sun; for their

steps

steps in thy presence was lovely; and before their time thou hast shone on Morven. And thou wilt remember them in the time to come, O sun, when this gray stone shall be sought in vain. Yes; for "thou wilt endure," said the bard of ancient days "after the moss of time shall grow in Temora; after the blast of years shall roll over the oaks of Selma.——

Tratha'.

Sulvina's

SULDINA's CLOON.

Come forth, sigh of woe. Roll down, tears of grief. Mourn the fall of the lovely. Bathe the memory of the white=armed daughter of Morald.——Why doth the wandering stream smile as it passeth? Why doth the finny tribe sport in the chrystal flood? Roll in darkness, ye glittering waves! Retire to the blackest pool, ye silver winged?——Sound no horn on my hills, ye followers of the stag! Spare the hide of the roe, ye bearers of the winged arrow!——Nod your green heads in grief, ye leafy daughters of the forest! Sing a tale of woe, ye tenants of the bush.———Why dost thou travel in thy mildness, soft breath of summer? The fairest flower that ever met thee is low. The friendship of the breeze shall no more smile on the cheek of the rose. The waving ringlets of her dark-brown hair shall no more tremble on the wings of the passing breeze.

Away with thy voice of Mirth, joyful morning! she, who was wont to shine before thy early beams, shall not awake. Hang your drooping heads, ye flowers of the mead! A surly blast hath plucked the fairest lilly from her stalk. Lonely is her dwelling in the gloomy tomb. The sun-beams of coming years shall not smile on her virgin charms.

But come, O come, with all thy sable clouds, black-robed night! Grasp the hills in thy dark bosom. Let the shrieks of ghosts, the screams of owls, and the course of meteors, be around me. —— Let the strength of the angry blast bear me on its wings; and let the spirits of the wind hum their tales of woe in my ear.

Come

Come forth from thy narrow dwelling in the land of graves, thou beam that wert lovely. Why didst thou retire in the midst of thy blooming years, like the midnight star, that rushes behind a dark cloud? The mariners home is near its bed in the western waves. His eager eyes search for it in vain among the boisterous billows, and blustering blasts of stormy night; but he finds it not.

Why dost thou pour the beams of thy kindness around me, bright queen of night? The friendship of thy smiles brings no joy to me. More welcome are the frowns of grizzly ghosts, the tremendous voice of bursting clouds, or the surly aspect of the watchful storm! Away with thy glaring light, insulting moon! Hide thyself among the dark folds of nightly clouds. Never shall your smiles call forth Sulvina from the hall: never shall your silent beams dance

round

round her graceful shadow. The form of her who was lovely shall no more wander along the rustling heath.——The meeting of warriors is in the hall of Morald; but the voice of mirth is not there. No white fingers are seen among the trembling strings. Mute is the harp. Loud are the sighs. What eye can refuse a tear to the lovely!

A cloud has darkened the valley at noon.——The sun=beam of my joy is set, no more to return. My eyes shall never more behold its coming forth from the back of the eastern hill.

Then, come, raven=haired night! with all thy black clouds. Spread thy drowsy wings over the inhabitants of the forest; and let the tenants of the cottage pursue their blisful dreams among the visionary mountains that rise near the couch of their slumbers: ——But talk not of sleep to me, gloomy night; my

breast

breast is the house of woe. Tho' thou rulest in darkness over the children of nature, I regard thee not. Wilt thou thyself rest, when the all-lightening sun shakes his white locks in the east: wilt thou then presume to combat the coming forth of his beauty?——No; thou fliest in haste with thy gathered clouds; and the wretched only mourn thy departure.——Where is the course of thy journey, black cloud? Rush in haste from thy dwelling in the sky. Bear me on the wings of thy strength: Bear me over boisterous seas, to distant isles, where the souls of the lovely rejoice before the sun-beams of eternal day.——

Do thou, Sulvina, meet me with the sweetest of thy smiles; and be the pillar of my wandering steps to the Isle of Peace.——

Cran=Mella

ORAN-MORIA.

No joy is mine in the absence of the maid of love. The white bosoms of a hundred virgins meet the sun-beams on the banks of Cormic: but thy equal, matchless maid of the rolling eye! is not there.—— Thy smiles are as the glances of the sire of brightness, when he rides in meredian splendor over the mountains. Thy words as the voice of many harps, when the songs of bards are heard, and their fingers travel among the trembling strings.

Thou art distant far, maid of Cormic! But dark mountains raise their cliffy heads between us in vain. Mine eyes shall never cease to view the image of the lovely. My thoughts shall wander round the crouding beauties that attend thee.

A a   The

The eager eyes of a hundred warriors are towards the captivating charms which adorn the swelling surface of thy rising bosom. The fairest lilly that shines in the forest, contends not with the sweetness of its smiles; and, when it meets the sun-beams at noon, the swan is ashamed of her downy breast, and hides it beneath the rising wave.

Thy delicate fingers trace not in vain the folds of the lawn. Thy needle gave birth to the spreading tree, that seems to bend beneath the load of yellow fruit,——But stretch, lovely maid! stretch forth thy hand in kindness to me, and I will breathe, in reality, that life which the sons of thy needle but seem to enjoy. Let the friendship of thy eyes shine around me, and I will flourish before their beams, like the vegetable tribes that rear their tender heads beneath the kindly breath of summer.

Who

Who shall convey to song the form of the maid who moves matchless over the mountains? Her smooth neck is the white bed of her golden tresses. Her flowing ringlets fall in sweet disorder over her ivory shoulders. Soft blue eyes roll beneath a small round arch.——Warriors melt before the strength of their beams.

Move on in thy majestic steps, maid of the mild-rolling eye! The blooming heath shall meet thy graceful shadow in gladness: The verdant plain shall wave their grassy locks, and smile as it passeth. Grace is in thy presence. Thy breath is as the scent of a flowery garden, when it pours its sweet odours on the wings of the breeze.

The tongue of thy songs is surrounded by the white formers of the ivory ring. The sound of thy voice is like the music of the wood, when the feathery tribes

rejoice

rejoice among the rustling leaves.——O thou who formest those excellencies which captivate the enraptured eyes of men! this is the work of thy hand; and we feel the strength of its power. What, then, must be thy own perfections, since the object who starts into existence at thy nod, is thus beautifully formed!

Raise, daughter of night! raise thy fair head in the east: be the guide of my lonely journey over the dusky mountains.

Though lonely, I wander by the stream, though mournful, my sigh mingles with the wind of the desart; the favour of thy bright eyes, fair maid, would cheer me, as the sun the hills, when he pours forth the strength of his beauty at noon, and shakes the snow from their heathy locks.

The

The OLD BARD's WISH.

O Place me by the side of the murmuring rill, that gently glides with downward-rolling pace! lay my head in the shade of the spreading branches, and be thy friendly beams, O sun! in kindnefs around me.——There at ease let my side embrace the green grafs on the bank of the flowery garb, and let me taste the friendship of the breeze as it pafses. Let my feet, bathed in the chrystal flood, feel the strugling efforts of the yielding stream in its hasty journey.

Let the lilly of purest complexion smile near me on the yielding stalk; and the trembling dew glitter on the waving locks of my verdant seat. Let my hand recline on the daisied turf, and let the fragrant thyme be the pillow of my leaning cheek.

Round

Round on the high erected brows of my glen, let the hawthorn spread its blooming boughs, and the little children of the bushes rejoice in the songs of their love, repeated by the invisible tenants of the rock.

——"But hark! I hear the steps of the hunter. O may the cry of thy hounds, and the sound of thy darts, thou bender of the yew, be often heard around my silent dwelling! My wonted joy, when the chace arose, shall then return, and the bloom of youth shall glow in my cheek that was faded.——The marrow in my bones shall revive, when I hear the sound of spears, the bound of dogs, and the twang of strings. ——With joy I shall spring up alive when they cry 'The stag is fallen!'

" I shall then meet the companions of my chace; the hound that followed me late and early. I shall see the hills that I loved to frequent, and the rocks that

were

were wont to answer to my cries. I shall see the cave that often received my steps from night; the cave where we often rejoiced around the flame of the oak. Their our feast of deer was spread; there Treig was our drink, and the murmur of its streams our song.—— Ghosts shrieked on their clouds, and the spirits of the mountains roared along their hollow streams: but no fear was ours; in the cave of our rock secure we lay. ——I shall see Scur-elda tower above the vale, where the welcome voice of the cuckow is early heard.——I shall see Gormal, with its thousand pines; I shall see it in all its green beauty, with its many roes and flights of fowl.——I shall see the isle of trees in the lake, with the red fruit nodding over the waves.—— I shall see Arden, chief of a thousand hills: its sides are the abode of deer, its top the habitation of clouds.——I see——but whither, gay vision, are thou fled? Thou hast left me to return no more.

Farewel

"Farewell then, my beloved hills; farewel, children of youth. With you it is summer still: but my winter is come: no spring, alas, is to succeed!

—"O place me by the green side of my stream; place the shell, and my father's shield, beside me in my narrow house.—Open, open, ye ghosts of my fathers! the hall where Ossian and Daol reside—The evening of my life is come, and the bard shall be found no more.

FINIS.

www.ingramcontent.com/pod-product-compliance
Lightning Source LLC
Chambersburg PA
CBHW030833270326
41928CB00007B/1036